God Cried

God Cried

Tony Clifton and
Catherine Leroy

QUARTET BOOKS

LONDON   MELBOURNE   NEW YORK

First published by Quartet Books Limited 1983
A member of the Namara Group
27/29 Goodge Street, London W1P 1FD

Copyright © 1983 by Tony Clifton and Catherine Leroy

Photographs on pages 138 and 139
courtesy Alain Mingam

British Library Cataloguing in Publication Data
Clifton, Tony
    God cried.
    1. Israel—Armed Forces   2. Beirut (Lebanon)—
    Bombardment, 1982   3. Lebanon—History—
    Civil War, 1975–
    I. Title   II. Leroy, Catherine
    956.92   DS89.B4

    ISBN 0-7043-2375-3

Typeset by MC Typeset, Chatham, Kent.
Printed and bound by Hazell Watson and Viney Ltd,
Aylesbury, Bucks.

For Bernard and Claire

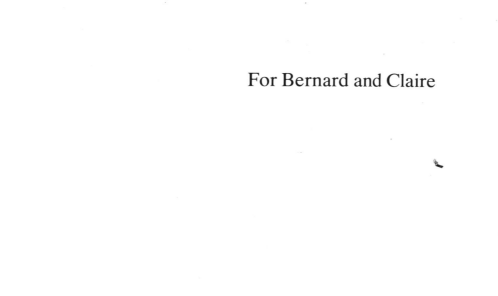

Contents

God Cried

Fatmeh Jaber — aged twelve

1
The Reasons Why

Official evil lives in the Middle East, and the ruins and graves of Beirut testify to its strength. But that evil was not triumphant in Beirut, and this story is about the people who beat it back.

This is a book about the most savage bombardment of a capital city since the end of the Second World War. It will not be much use as a textbook about the Israeli siege of west Beirut because it is very short on dates and exact times and contains very few quotations from important people and official documents. Right at the beginning, it should be said that *God Cried* is not objective and could never have been. It is in the nature of sieges that you have to be on one side or the other, and that has been so since the first man to build a wall watched the second one try to break through it. Our story comes from inside the perimeter, from among the Lebanese and the Palestinians who chose – or were forced – to live and fight and die in those few blood-soaked square miles in the summer of 1982.

When you are stuck right in the middle of a war, it is almost impossible to make up your mind about the real meaning of what you see happening around you. Most of your waking hours are spent simply recording the events of the day; you surf through the time on a wave of adrenalin, generated partly by fear, partly by excitement and partly by journalistic competitiveness; rushing from burning building to hospital to front line; filling sweat-soaked and dust-stained notebooks with almost unreadable writing. You have to meet deadlines and answer endless queries from editors; you have to wrestle with a communications system likely at any time to be cut by shelling or Israeli technicians anxious to stop you telling your story. When you do finish for the day, you don't change mental gears into a more reflective mood, sit back and consider the implications of what you have just

seen; the flood of hormones drives you into the bar where you re-live the day with your friends and get drunk, or to the restaurant where you do the same thing . . . only it takes longer in the restaurant because the staple roast beef and jacket potatoes soak up some of the booze. When you do get to bed you can't sleep unless you're stoned out of your mind, you can't wind down quickly enough before the early morning barrage ends your half-sleep and propels you into the streets again. You're never really tired because the drama of events keeps you wide awake, but you're in an entirely different mode from what you're used to, and when you do write, the words don't come out as measured observations but in a flood as involuntary as sweat. When you finish, you pick up the pages and you have to read through them to see what you have just written. If you work for *The Times,* you record the events of the day; if you work for *Newsweek,* you go through the events of the week. The length of your attention span is the length of your deadline; each day and each week is so filled with incident that you simply haven't time or space to refer to happenings outside that time span, unless to use them briefly as reference points for what you are writing at the moment, as in '. . . the bombing of the camps on Wednesday was the heaviest since the raids of two weeks ago'.

You don't have time to put the past in context, and you know it is futile to try to predict what will happen next: you have no control over events and your view of what is happening is totally one-sided, because in a war you cannot flit from one side to the other. You console yourself by reasoning that as a journalist, you are not there to give an overall view; your job is to report your own little world and leave it to someone else to report the little world existing on the other side with the batteries that are now pouring fire down on you. You live from deadline to deadline, and you suspend judgement on the grand question of what it all means. When the war is over, you think, you will be able to stand back and look at what happened from all angles: you will read the stories from the other side, you will read the reports of the neutral observers, and finally you will understand the reason why the things that happened to you did happen.

Beirut was not the first city in which I have found myself besieged but the fourth. In Dacca in 1971 there was no trouble in deciding what was happening: the Indian army was marching in to break the power of the Pakistani army and allow the native Bengalis to set up their independent state of Bangladesh. In Pnom Penh in 1975, the objective of the Khmer Rouge was to overthrow the American-backed government and set up a communist regime. In Saigon, the North Vietnamese had a similar objective. But what were the Israelis really trying to do?

I suppose the best way to answer that is to let the people who did it explain why. Ariel Sharon, until very recently the Israeli Defence Minister, should know; when he was asked what it was all about, he told the Israeli Commission of Inquiry into the massacres in the Palestinian camps in Beirut: 'On 6 June 1982, we set out on a defensive war against the organizations of terror of the P.L.O.'

If that's true, it's an admission that in 1982 the armed forces of Israel suffered the most humiliating defeat in their history. At the end of August 1982, 'the organizations of terror of the P.L.O.' marched, undefeated, out of Beirut with their guns over their shoulders and the head terrorist, Yasser Arafat, took a healthful sea-cruise down the Mediterranean to a hero's welcome in Athens. The best-equipped army in the Middle East, supported by one of the most powerful air forces in the world, backed by a navy, and outnumbering its opponents by a conservative five to one, was totally unable to knock off a band of ragged-arsed kids equipped with the sort of weapons that might just about control a football crowd in Uruguay . . . and they didn't have any sort of a navy or air force, either.

Well, it's possible, isn't it? I mean, you can't win all the time . . . Look at Spurs in the Milk Cup in 1983. There they were, up near the top of the First Division in the English Football League, and they got beaten 4–1 by Burnley, who were propping up the Second Division. You wouldn't get a result like that once in fifty years. Maybe it was the same with the Israelis: they just had one of those off-years that even the best armies have from time to time. It's a funny game, is war.

As I said at the beginning, this is not a history of the war in Lebanon in 1982 – but the invasion does need to be put in some sort of context. While it was actually happening around me I had no difficulty at all in deciding what the Israelis were up to: they were going to bombard Beirut until everyone in it was dead or unable

to stop them breaking into the city. Then I got out in one piece and went back to London, and after a month there I decided that wasn't what it was about at all; what they were doing was consolidating their colonization of Lebanon by destroying its capital and its commercial heart. Four months later, as I actually start writing, I have junked the two early theories and come up with another which I will try to explain in about three paragraphs. I don't need any more because I don't have to prove anything legally, with quotations and documents to back me up. The Israeli government will confirm or knock down my case for me.

I have reached the spooky conclusion that the war in Lebanon had almost nothing to do with the Palestinians or the Lebanese. I've read as much as I can about recent events in Israel, I've watched television and I've talked to the pundits; I've come to the conclusion that the destruction of half of Lebanon, the killing of 25,000 civilians and the deaths of at least 500 Israeli soldiers were the results of a diversionary action . . . So cheer up, all you bereaved mothers and fathers and children, daddy and mummy and Uncle Mohammed and Cousin Shlomo didn't die for anything serious.

To boil the history down, Menachem Begin needed to divert the world's attention from the fact that he was taking over the occupied West Bank of the River Jordan and making it an integral part of Israel. The way he is doing this is by having his government build vast numbers of housing settlements on the West Bank and filling them with Jewish settlers, so that what was once an almost purely Arab section of the area will become as Jewish as Tel Aviv. He had to shovel those people into what he calls 'Judaea and Samaria' as fast as possible because the Americans and Europeans and the other Arabs had at last got their act together to the point at which they realized that if the Palestinians didn't get some sort of homeland soon, their howling and screaming and shooting were going to destabilize an area where a lot of the world's oil is stored. And that trio of interests had made it clear to everyone that the only logical place to have a 'Palestinian entity' was where the Palestinians already were and had always been – and that is on the West Bank.

Well, someone is almost certain to notice that something's up if you suddenly start a building programme designed to house 100,000 Jews in an area as small as the West Bank. This will all be achieved in only three years; it means that if you live in somewhere like Hebron, one day you can look out of your window and see the bare rock that Christ once walked over, and the next you can see nothing but concrete cubes decorated with blue-and-white flags and dominated by the brooding outline of the Menachem Begin Memorial Kindergarten and Artillery School. The cubes are spreading like herpes now, but the disease might not have started if anyone had been on the lookout for symptoms in 1982. They weren't, because world powers have the brains of hungry crocodiles: too small to take in more than one event at a time, but developed enough to observe that event with single-minded concentration (just watch a crocodile stalk a drinking gazelle one day). Last year, the crocodile's attention was fixed first on the Falklands; when that disappeared, the movement that next attracted its eye was the invasion of Lebanon. Now its great armour-plated head is turning away from Lebanon and slowly focusing on the West Bank; but it is far too late. If the messiah decided to make a comeback in the traditional manner today, he would find that the inn had been demolished to make way for a superhighway from Tel Aviv and the manger flattened to make way for a Gush Emunim settlement.

I arrived at this conclusion – that the Lebanon invasion was a cover-up by adopting the Sherlock Holmes principle: you eliminate everything that doesn't stand up to proof and what is left is the truth, however improbable it may be. So it was with the invasion. Sharon says that the Israelis went to Beirut in a defensive war against the organizations of terror of the P.L.O. Well the P.L.O. left Beirut as an intact fighting force and with its entire leadership undamaged; they are already back in action, killing Israeli soldiers in south Lebanon and around Beirut. I left Beirut with the greatest admiration for the fighting qualities both of the Palestinians and of the Lebanese and Syrians who fought with them; but I have to say that I believe that if Israel had really gone all-out, they would have broken into west Beirut because they commanded an overwhelming amount of firepower. But they would also have had to accept thousands, rather than hundreds, of deaths – and this they were not prepared to do. The reason was not just a failure of will, but because the taking of Beirut and the destruction of the P.L.O. was basically irrelevant to the Israeli masterplan. What they wanted was to conduct the most violent war possible while themselves taking as few casualties and as much time as possible. I'm sure they would love to have knocked off the P.L.O. as a bonus, but they weren't prepared to pay a high price to make it a certainty.

After I had decided that the Israelis weren't out to get the P.L.O., I thought for a short time that the invasion was really an Israeli takeover of Lebanon and that the attack was launched to create a sort of 'North Bank' that would give Israel the valuable waters of Lebanon's River Litani and also the very rich orchards and tobacco farms of the south. This theory can be half proved, because the Israelis now do occupy the south and they are currently telling the Lebanese in the 'peace talks' between the two countries that if they, the Israelis, pull out, they will demand in return the right to erect a line of heavily armed observation posts strung across the south, each manned by about 600 soldiers. But if the Israelis wanted to keep the south (which they took with minimal casualties), why did they go on to Beirut, where they lost most of their 500 dead and spent about $2 billion? They

didn't take Beirut so why did they go? The reason has to be that they took only a week to clean up the south . . . and that wasn't long enough for their real plan. They set up a siege – a tactic quite foreign to a go get 'em army like the I.D.F. – because it was the only way they could stretch Beirut's highly diverting death agonies into months.

They prolonged the torture by a clever mixture of war and diplomacy. To use the first they would say, launch a savage bombing raid on one of the Palestinian camps. The Palestinian defenders would fire back, so the Israelis would redouble the assault, on the grounds that the Palestinians were attacking *them* and they were justified in firing back in self-defence. They used diplomacy by quibbling over every tiny detail in any ceasefire proposal suggested by the Lebanese the Palestinians or the Americans led by Philip Habib – as I describe in detail later on, one day they even objected to the use of the initial 'D' in the name of one proposal. They jerked poor old Phil Habib from Jerusalem to east Beirut like a demented yoyo, sometimes encouraging him by some hint of concession, at other times flattening him with an outright refusal to stop the killing. All the reporters in Beirut came to hate the 'peace talks', because editors back home never understood what was going on; we would be cowering in the hotel basement as splinters rained down on the road outside, when the telex would break into life: it would be some mastermind in Chicago or Los Angeles demanding to know what Habib had had for breakfast before his latest triumph. In the end, the people who weren't there made Habib into the greatest peacemaker since Francis of Assisi; but in fact he was as helpless as the rest of us; he got the plaudits just because he happened to be around when Begin and company decided that they'd achieved what they had set out to do. Begin was not stopped by a phone call from President Reagan, or by a piece of Habib diplomacy: he ended the war because he had got what he wanted, just as a rapist stops humping after he has had his orgasm. By the time the Israelis called it a day, the West Bank was well on its way to being welded to Israel for as long as Israel exists.

As I say, the Israeli government will prove me right or wrong because by the time this book is published, the West Bank takeover will be irreversible – or they will have agreed to hand over the West Bank to the Palestinians to allow them to join in a federation with Jordan, which is what President Reagan wants. But I write all this without any qualms. Like a good little reporter, I interrupted this paragraph in mid-sentence to listen to the B.B.C. news of 30 January, and there was Menachem Begin providing me with the next few lines. He has been talking at a fund-raising dinner in Jerusalem and has just told his audience that it was the 'inalienable right' of Jews to settle there because 'the West Bank is part of the land of your forefathers'; he went on in the nicest possible way to tell President Reagan where to put his federated state by saying, 'the prospect of a Palestinian state on the West Bank is a mortal danger which must be avoided at any cost'.

The problem for anyone who lives within bombing distance of the state of Israel is that, when Menachem Begin talks about 'any cost', he is not talking about any cost to Israel and its people, but any cost to people or countries that might interfere with his plans. Lebanon is the latest to foot the bill for Israeli expansionism; although the figures will never be accurate, because too many people were either buried in rubble or literally disintegrated by explosions, it seems that a minimum of 25,000 people were killed and at least 30,000 wounded in the invasion of Lebanon, and about one-third of those casualties were inflicted on the people caught in west Beirut. All the sources I have seen, from Lebanese police to Red Cross officials and doctors and nurses, agree that eighty per cent of the casualties were civilian. Today there are about 300,000 people, mainly Palestinians from the ruined camps, who are homeless and the estimate for the cost of repairing the damage in the ruined cities, as given by the new Lebanese President Amin Gemayel is $7 billion, with $3 billion needed for Beirut alone. Not bad for a military diversion.

Somehow I don't see the generals and cabinet ministers of Israel writing the sort of triumphant books about 'Operation Peace For Galilee' that followed the Six Day War and the Yom Kippur War. Do you get medals in the Israeli army for burning off women's faces with phosphorus bombs; do Israeli bomber pilots paint tiny silhouettes of hospitals on the fuselages of their planes, as British aces used to put up swastikas for German planes downed? Will General Rafael Eitan come up with his memoirs called *Beirut Victory,* or Ariel Sharon with something on the lines of *The Man Who Smashed the P.L.O.*? There will be books, but those to make an impact will be ones like *The Longest War,* the book about the invasion by Jacobo Timmerman, the Argentinian Jew who was once imprisoned and tortured by the fascist regime in Argentina and who now wonders whether Menachem Begin is trying to take his adopted country Israel down the same path the Argentinian generals chose. It must be one of the greatest ironies of his extraordinary life that, having escaped from an anti-semitic country, Timmerman ended up in another nation led by one of the greatest living anti-Semites. Menachem Begin is after all the leader of a country whose armed forces last year alone, killed 25,000 members of a semitic race, the Arabs who live in Lebanon.

My author friends all advised me to leave this first chapter until the last, so that I would be able to re-read what I had written and lay out my major conclusions for the reader who is about to plough into the pages that follow. My first conclusion is that this book could not have been published without Catherine's pictures, because many things happened that were almost impossible to describe just in words, and other things occurred which people would not believe unless they had the pictorial evidence in front of them.

It took me about three seconds to reach the conclusion that I needed Catherine much more than she needed me . . . but it is now clear that nothing else is going to crystallize with such certainty before I reach my deadline. All around me I have a pile of crumpled paper bearing a lot of half-arsed and sentimental paragraphs about the kindness of the people of west Beirut who looked after me, even though I worked for an American magazine and we were being fired on by hardware originating in America. I wrote that the bravest people in the whole of the city were the Lebanese civilians who refused to leave even when they had the chance, because they weren't going to be kicked out of their homes by foreign invaders. And I started to say something about hope for peace being generated by the hundreds of thousands of Israelis who demonstrated against the war.

But I finally tore up all that stuff because I couldn't see that it was going anywhere – in the sense that there was not going to be peace even though good and brave people on both sides of the Lebanon–Israel border wanted it. In fact just as I was near to finishing this chapter two events occurred which although 'good' in isolation, will probably only serve to help the current Israeli government realize its long-term plan of absorbing the West Bank and making southern Lebanon an Israel-controlled territory. The first event was the deportation of the Nazi mass-murderer Klaus Barbie to France from Bolivia; the second was the publication of the Kahan Report, the official inquiry into the massacre of the Palestinians in the Sabra and Chatila camps of Beirut in September 1982. The thought that two such disparate events, one a cause of agony for all Jews and the second a condemnation by Israeli judges of the Begin government, will almost certainly help Menachem Begin, makes me wonder sometimes if there is not some demonic angel taking special care of him.

The trial of Barbie, 'the Butcher of Lyons', will inevitably mean dredging up the stories of Barbie's persecution of the Jews and non-Jews of Lyons when he was head of the Gestapo there during the war; it will doubtless concentrate especially on the transportation of forty-one Jewish children from an orphanage which Barbie as he himself put it, 'cleaned out' by sending the children to their deaths in Auschwitz in 1944. While the bare earth is still fresh and red over the graves of the hundreds of children killed in Beirut by the Israelis and their allies in 1982, the world's attention will be diverted to the fate of those long-dead children, and the evidence of their suffering will be used by Israel's militarists to justify their own killings of 1982. Jewish children, we will be told in one way or another, must 'never again' suffer as they once did – although the rider 'even if other people's children must suffer tenfold', will not be heard.

But while an ancient and evil Nazi will be subjected to his richly deserved prosecution in Lyons, the men who planned and authorized the destruction and wholesale slaughter of civilians in Lebanon in 1982 will almost certainly find that their actions actually benefit their careers. The supreme irony is: this will happen because of the publication in Jerusalem of the findings of the Kahan Inquiry – which hardly spares the reputation of a single member of that team which had decided that the destruction of Lebanon was to be their major good deed for 1982.

The Kahan Inquiry was confined to determining the role and responsibilities of the Israeli armed forces and their military and civilian commanders in the massacre of the Palestinians in the Beirut camps by Christian gunmen and it didn't spare its own people. Begin they concluded, didn't really bother about what was likely to happen if the Christians were allowed into west Beirut, nor did he make much effort to find out what was happening. Ariel Sharon bore 'personal responsibility' and should resign or be fired from the post of Defence Minister. The Chief of Staff General Rafael Eitan, knew what was happening, as did the Director of Military Intelligence Major-General Yehoshua Saguy, and the Beirut Divisional Commander Brigadier Amos Yaron. Eitan they decided, was not worth punishing because his military career was about to end anyway with his retirement, but they wanted Saguy fired and Yaron relieved of a field command for the next three years. My Palestinian friends were unimpressed by what the Kahan Inquiry decided, because they couldn't understand how Begin had escaped the harshest condemnation on the grounds that he was the overall leader of this callous crew. I was more impressed, mainly by the honesty of the report and partly because I had just had to study a similar report in Britain, that of the Franks Commission into the origins of the Falklands war. Where the Franks team had gone out of its way to use every nitpicking legal nicety to produce 106 pages of pap which told the British voter very little and blamed nobody for failing to foresee a war which had been predicted in the Argentine papers with the same ballyhoo as the opening of *E.T.,* Kahan cut through the legal bullshit to produce not a legal but a moral judgement which states at one point in its conclusion: '. . . but the end never justifies the means, and basic ethical and human values must be maintained in the use of arms'.

The rest of this book is about what happened to a city and its people when a group of Israel's military and civilian leaders decided that an end really did justify a means. The book is due to appear by the middle of 1983; if the pundits both inside and outside Israel are right, at this time most of the men condemned by the Kahan Report will be savouring further triumphs. Begin will be Prime Minister and it is likely that he will use his increasing popularity with his country's Sephardic majority to call an early election and be returned with a bigger majority. Sharon had to resign as Defence Minister but, despite massive protests he has been kept on in the cabinet as Minister without Portfolio and has just been appointed to government sub-committees dealing with defence and the West Bank – a classic case of the wolf being put in charge of the sheep. If there is an early election he and Eitan will probably move into one of the extreme right-wing parties that are blooming like flesh-eating orchids in Israel and will probably be big men in the next Begin coalition. The Kahan judges who sought to lay some sort of a reprimand on that gruesome trio will discover that the current perverse direction of Israeli nationalism has turned their condemnatory judgement into a glowing endorsement.

When I read back over these last few paragraphs I find it hard not be deeply depressed. The moral of the siege of Beirut would seem to be that if you are cruel and brutal enough you will get what you want and the world will either reward you or, at least, not stand in your way. So far might has triumphed spectacularly in Lebanon by giving right a resounding kick in the groin while the referee wasn't looking. But if one people's special claim to rightness and bravery died outside Beirut, those same qualities blossomed in another group of people inside that poor battered city in 1982. And this story is about the insiders.

Downtown Beirut, 1976

2
Shared Misery

I never knew Beirut in the good old days that the pre-1975 people talk about. I never swam in the morning and skied in the afternoon, I never saw Ella Fitzgerald sing at the Baalbek Festival. The 'Switzerland of the Middle East', where Muslim, Christian and Jew worked and played together in perfect harmony was before my time. I got there just as the city and my own career were coming apart in August 1975. I was in trouble because I'd screwed up reporting the Khmer Rouge takeover of Cambodia, because in the end I was unable to convince myself until weeks after everyone else that those nice gentle Cambodians could do such terrible things to one another. Beirut (and Lebanon, for that matter) was in trouble because the inequalities written into the constitution had pushed Muslims into considering using their guns to get their democratic rights, and Christians into thinking about using guns to defend their privileges. My own troubles were made very clear to me by the *Newsweek* Beirut bureau chief at the time, an old friend called Nick Proffitt, who had been asked to break it to me as gently as possible that there were some difficulties with my recent work. 'Shit, man, you got cancer. Everyone back in New York says you better start looking for a new job before this one runs out on you.'

I was so down in those first few weeks that I never did the things I would like to have done. They weren't important, but the opportunity has gone, along with the places. It was a time of a sort of phoney peace; there had been very serious riots and shoot-outs between Muslims and Christians in the early part of the year but nothing big enough to suggest we were on the brink of a civil war. If I hadn't been thinking about going back to Australia and phoning friends in Fleet Street to ask if there were any jobs going, I would have had a drink in the bar at the St George's Hotel, watched the topless girls and the

elephants in the floor-show at the Casino du Liban and walked through the covered *souks* in the old Turkish centre of the city. I suppose there's a gap in my life because I didn't know the Beirut where Kim Philby drank; but I don't regret it because I never knew it. The civil war broke out in earnest about a month after I arrived, so my Beirut is the city of massacres and gunfights and bombings, of crazy booze and hash sessions with my fellow hacks, and of endless arguments with Lebanese about why the war had started and with Palestinians about how and when they were going to get a homeland. I don't miss the good old days because I hardly brushed shoulders with them, and anyway the war washed away a lot of the bullshit that was thickly encrusted on Beirut. Most of the social butterflies, what the local English-language paper used to call 'all of *le tout* Beirut', fluttered off to Paris and London and down to the Gulf when the war began again; the ones who stayed believed (for the right or wrong reasons) that they had a stake in the country and were going to fight to defend it. The civil war changed everything in Lebanon and in the context of this book, it trained people for the siege of 1982 and enabled me to get to know the Palestinians as well as I think I got to know the Lebanese.

Knowing the Palestinians was much more difficult before the civil war. By that I don't mean that you couldn't meet Palestinians; they were all over the place and the universities and newspapers and business wouldn't have run without them. By the Palestinians I mean the cadres in the Palestine Liberation Organization and their members. Before 1975 they were everyone's bad guys because they went round hijacking planes, shooting up airports and assassinating Israeli civilians. They were doubly damned by most reporters, not only because they were terrorists *per se*, but because their terrorist acts were directed against the Israelis who at that time were universally regarded as honest and chivalrous and, above all, the democratic defenders of decency in the Middle East. Before the civil war began and the Palestinians came in on the leftist/Muslim Lebanese side, news reporters and the P.L.O. had a difficult relationship, because neither really trusted the other or liked what it was doing. Pre-civil-war reporting saw most events in the Middle East as Israel (good) versus Arab (from not-so-good to terrible, depending on whether you were talking about the Saudis or the P.L.O.). The P.L.O. people didn't see any point in talking to reporters who saw them all as blood-crazed terrorists.

word 'Christian' for want of a better catch-all term; the point about east Beirut is that there was no real Muslim presence there after the nastiness began. As people soon found out, enjoying a thoroughly good bombardment together does tend to bind people closer, if only in shared misery. So the realization began to grow that the Palestinians probably did belong somewhere in the human race . . . out on the edges maybe, just in a little way from the marmosets and lemurs, but definitely not out there with the vampire-bats and puff-adders where they had been classified before.

Secondly, because at this stage there were no Israelis involved, the Pals could be seen in the round, as a people, as a political entity and as a military force, rather

Beirut, 1976

The civil war changed the relationship for ever. For a start geography played its part: it so happened that the west of Beirut where the embassies were and where the reporters all lived, was the 'Muslim' part of the city – though naming it so is not strictly accurate because there were always a lot of Christians in west Beirut and they stayed through the war; but when the city split into opposing halves, reporters and Palestinians (and about 750,000 other people as well) all found themselves huddling together under Christian bombardment. I use the

than as a mindless cancer attacking the pure body of Israel. Reporters discovered that they could quote a Palestinian spokesman saying, 'The Phalangists killed 2,000 people at Tal Zaatar', and not have questions from New York or London offices about whether or not this was true . . . something that would nearly always happen if you quoted a Palestinian source accusing the Israelis of an atrocity. The Palestinians found they were being treated like people and quoted without qualifying phrases suggesting they were pathological liars; they began to trust the reporters and give them the sort of access that would have been unthinkable before the war. When I got to Beirut in 1975, a man like Bassam abu Sharif of the Popular Front for the Liberation of Palestine was placed in the category of blood-crazed terrorist considerably to the left of the Antichrist. By the time I left, after the Israelis had finished with Beirut in 1982, he was a straightforward spokesman for the Palestinians who if anything was too moderate when describing massacres on television.

The civil war cured my professional cancer: after I emerged from the end of the fighting in 1978 I had rehabilitated myself . . . written lots of 'I was there' stories, got shelled, tied up and threatened with death,

stopped the Israelis in their tracks. Then the Israelis set up their puppet regime with Major Saad Haddad in charge of south Lebanon, and went back home to Tel Aviv or wherever. So once again I said goodbye to all my friends, to Harry the optician and Abed at the squash courts and Souha at the 'If' boutique and Mahmoud at the P.L.O. and Abdul in the office, and returned to London to write about Margaret Thatcher, and then to Iran for the fall of the Shah and the taking of the American Embassy and . . . anyway I'll write a book about it one day.

I was sitting in London in June 1982, pondering the British economy and trying to psych myself up for yet another piece about how Thatcher was surging ahead

got some nice interviews with Arafat, written some pieces I liked about the way the city and its people were being fucked over and yet were still surviving . . . split a prize for it all, and gone back to London. I arrived in London around March of 1978 and was sent straight back to Lebanon because the Israelis had just begun their first invasion of the south. So I spent a couple of months down near the Israeli border, watching the air-strikes and hiding with the guerrillas in the orange groves and listening to their stories about how they'd

despite rising unemployment, when suddenly I saw all this Lebanese war stuff on the television. Very strange, sitting there watching those dusty yellow Israeli tanks rolling up the familiar roads of south Lebanon, the bursts of fire, the explosions in the little concrete block-houses, the Palestinian kids sitting by the road, hands tied and blindfolded. It's funny, that Israeli thing about blindfolding prisoners. Clearly they're not going to see anything secret on the side of a road even if they have their eyes open, and it's harder to move blindfolded men

19

around because they keep falling over; but it's all part of the tactic of keeping people frightened and uncertain. The image to the whole world of the blindfolded man, long before the invasion of Lebanon, is of the man about to be executed, tied to a lamp-pole in Liberia, or hanged from a lamp-post in the Jewish ghettos of Eastern Europe, or standing up facing the guns like the Kurds taken prisoner by Khomeini's teenage hit-men in Iran. The blindfold frightens the man wearing it and terrifies his family and the people who see him stumbling away.

It's hard to analyse why I felt I had to go back to see for myself what was happening. Glory was a factor naturally; if you're in the newspaper reporting business you want to be where the best story is, and there's no question that this was it, because it just naturally filled the huge hole left on the front pages by the end of the Falklands war. But glory wasn't the only factor, because I wasn't all that sorry about having missed the Falklands – and I know I would have broken a leg rather than go to El Salvador, even when it was the only war worth attending. What drew me to Lebanon this time (apart from my old war-horse reactions) was that I felt this was going to be a climactic time in the history of both the Lebanese and the Palestinians, and I had too many good friends in both groups to be away from them when their future was being decided. I'm glad I was sent into west Beirut to be with 'my' people as well; I would have gone in on the Israeli side if I'd had to, because there was a fascinating story to be done on how the Israeli soldiers coped with what they were having to do; but I would have felt very uncomfortable, like being with the South Africans on a raid into Lesotho or Angola. It would have been very hard to sit with the Israeli tank commanders and gunners and watch them firing down into a city I loved and at people who had been my friends for almost a decade. Looking back on those two months in 1982 I am profoundly thankful I was there; I would have felt a real sense of loss if I'd had to stand around in years to come and listen to other people telling how they'd survived the siege of Beirut. I have that feeling now when I hear people talk about the fall of Saigon. I had reported that war on and off for five years – and I took a holiday two weeks before the North Vietnamese walked in. I can still hardly bear to hear good friends like Stewart Dalby and Catherine talk about what it was like to be there when the city finally fell. Your motives for doing these things are very complex: you want to show you're the bravest guy on the block, you want the 'I was there' glory, and you want to be with your friends when they're in the shit, so that if things go wrong you'll be able to make sure that their passing doesn't go unrecorded.

It was slightly surreal, sitting there in London in those early days of July, watching the Israelis knocking hell out of west Beirut on T.V. every night and wondering how people could survive . . . and knowing that I would be going there soon. In a sense it always looks worse on television: the people running in terror, the buildings

crumbling, the blood running down the faces of people staggering away from car-bombs. The television guys aren't going to intercut with shots of hacks standing around having a Veuve Clicquot in the bar at night, so it all looks like unrelieved horror.

I had one of those introductions to the war that didn't happen to Ernest Hemingway. Got into Damascus late

Assault course, Chiyah 1975

at night and was told by the driver we would be leaving at four-thirty in the morning so we wouldn't get to Beirut after dark, when it was dangerous. Oh yes, and we were taking an Armenian reporter's seventy-three-year-old aunt down there as well – her son's wife had left to be safe and she had come back to the Middle East so she would be able to look after him. For Christ's sake, here's the famous war correspondent, veteran of battles from Biafra to Ban Me Thuot, and he's going to war with somebody's seventy-three-year-old aunt. As it turned out, it was useful to have the old dear with us because at half the checkpoints they saw the nice old lady in the front seat and assumed that the lies my driver was telling – about me taking her to east Beirut for medical treatment because she had cancer – were true. There we were, poncing off in the direction of war, me in the back with my typewriter hidden under a blanket, old Mrs Hagopian (or whatever her name was) sitting bolt upright beside Atin, the driver, and Atin (who was also Armenian and spoke very few words of any known language) occasionally turning back to me and saying reassuringly, 'No program, no program.'

As it happened it was a quiet day: I think the Israelis had probably been belting the Syrians the day before, or it was the Sabbath or Menachem Begin's birthday. Anyway, the Syrians in their preposterous bright-pink mottled camouflage suits – a colour presumably devised by their Russian military advisers so they would be easily visible from 20,000 feet to the pilot of an Israeli F-16 – were lolling about at their checkpoints as we drove down one side of the slope into the Beka'a Valley in eastern Lebanon and up the other side of the hills that eventually roll on to Beirut. No aerial activity, the Syrian tank-crews lying back on their dug-in tanks, the occasional lethargic checkpoint guard waving us on – funny how the guys at the checkpoints all looked like President Assad, right down to the moustaches and the military haircuts covered by the little pill-box-shaped forage caps like Assad almost always wore when he appeared in uniform. So there we were, motoring along taking in the sights, me getting nostalgic about the views down into the valleys below, thinking about all that good hash just up the road in Baalbek, Mrs Whateverhernamian gazing stolidly ahead and Atin the driver still assuring me that we weren't going to have any kind of a program getting to Beirut.

Well, not much. Eventually we got through the Syrian lines at Sofar, which was once a pretty mountain resort where rich Gulf Arabs and a few locals had summer mansions, and which is now very much second-hand because of the war and we were coming up the hill when we hit the end of a huge line of cars. So I got out of our car and walked all the way up the hill, and there at the top like spiders at the centre of a web (it was a major crossing where about five roads, all clogged with cars, crossed one another), was the Israeli army, this time in the form of two extremely bored young privates sitting in

the middle of this huge traffic jam that they had caused simply by putting barbed wire across all the roads . . . two of them, sitting in the shade of their jeep, cradling their Galil rifles, clearly without a program in the world.

When I enumerate what I like least about the Israelis, their arrogant indifference to other races comes high on my list. This seemed to be a totally arbitrary roadblock aimed at disrupting traffic as much as possible because it was at a major junction. I asked the two if we could go through. A bored 'No'. Asked why. 'Because no one is going through.' Then could I see the commanding officer to explain I was a journalist and wanted to report the war? 'Yes, he can give you a paper.' Well, can I cross the wire to get to his office? 'No, you can't cross, you have to go round' – arm sweeps in an arc that takes in most of the mountains and ends up pointing roughly in the direction of Jerusalem. Owner of arm then slouches back against jeep.

So we took the long way round, and drove north about as far as Greece, and then turned towards the coast, so after about twelve hours instead of the usual three and a half we got to the Museum Crossing patrolled at one end by the Israelis and Christians, and by the Palestinians and Lebanese at the other. This was the famous 'green line' between east and west Beirut, the one-way valve that let through journalists and old Armenian women and anyone else silly enough to go from east to west. It didn't work as easily the other way: if you were Lebanese and had the papers to prove it, they let you out; if you were Palestinian of any kind, old woman, mother with child . . . just forget it – you stayed in west Beirut for the duration and waited for the next Israeli assault.

I don't think I knew anyone who, driving or walking from east to west Beirut, didn't feel the tension evaporate as soon as he got out of the Israeli–Christian sector. Here you were, you dumb idiot, walking into an area that's having the shit knocked out of it every day and night, and you're relieved. On the Christian side there was deep suspicion of anyone who wanted to go to west Beirut. You had to be either some kind of a Palestinian sympathizer or a spy or a smuggler, or you were one of those journalists who were going to write lies about Operation Peace For Galilee and the heroic efforts the Israeli brothers were making to free the western part of the city from the iron fist (heel? jackboot?) of the Palestinian invader. Your back tensed as you drove through the Christian lines, and you didn't relax until you got round the first earthwork barrier on the western side. There you were nearly always made welcome, on the all-happy-in-adversity-together principle. If you were fool enough to get into this shit with them, they were happy to have you on board.

It must have been about 5 p.m. when I got to the Commodore. Much yelling of welcome, hugging, hand-shaking, kissing various bristly Lebanese friends, running into the bar for the first cold Heineken of a long day. People standing around, Aspel and Fifi, Riggins, Nundy, Hajjaj, having a few cold ones, telling tales of amazing exploits, fantasizing about Julie Flint of U.P.I., wondering if the phones and telexes were going to be up that night. All presided over by the proprietor Yusef Nazzal, who is a multi-millionaire and chooses to stay in this dump, as he himself calls it, maybe because the staff would leave if he left, more likely because he's pretty bored with making money and life at the Commodore is never boring. I sat around and listened to the talk, everyone topping everyone else's stories about how close they came to death or to an interview with Arafat, or how they got this great stuff of this car-bomb blowing away forty-three people, and how those cretins in New York had once again cut all the references to 'indiscriminate shelling', on the grounds that the Israelis would never do anything as nasty as shell a city indiscriminately. After all, Israel was a small democratic country in a sea of Arab totalitarianism, and knew it had its standards to uphold . . . not that a church or hospital might not have taken a round – but none of it was on purpose or, if it was, it was because the Palestinians were hiding men or guns or ammunition there.

I ended the day in the exotically prosaic way I seemed to end most days in Beirut: drinking cold champagne, having a few tokes of hash to relax and playing game after game of darts with the English television crewmen. I went to bed about 1 a.m. and was wide awake at 5. I have to hand it to the Israelis, the buggers wake you in style. One minute you're out absolutely cold, flattened by the champagne, Valium and hash – and the next second (without any intervening voluntary action) you are cowering under the windowsill, the sky outside is brilliant with orange-red flares, and the enormous shock-waves of exploding shells are rattling the windows.

My room overlooked the swimming pool and faced eastwards, so the flares were lighting a morning bombardment of the perimeter where Christian east meets Muslim west Beirut. The flares descend slowly on their parachutes, swinging gently in the morning breeze and dripping incandescent white ash. I think they look like fireworks, but Abdul Hajjaj who has worked with us for years in Beirut, is completely spooked by them. 'I know it's ridiculous, but I lie awake all night when they use them because I can't help thinking one is going to blow through the window and burn the place down.' We all have different phobias. John Bulloch of the *Daily Telegraph* hates naval gunfire, because it's so random: there's Captain Bloom out there in his gunboat and he shoves a shell down the breech and just as he aims, a wave hits the ship and instead of blowing away the P.L.O. information office it drops on Bulloch. We know the guns are supposed to be stabilized against that sort of thing, but it doesn't help. My own fear is of car-bombs because the Christians and Israelis used them a lot in Beirut and they are totally random. You could be in Beirut, walking down any street, past any car on a totally peaceful day, and the next minute you could be torn to unrecognizable shreds by 500 pounds of *plastique* turning a car into two tons of shrapnel. Pieces of meat literally fly into the trees, and the blood sprays a hundred yards. After I have been close to the results of more than a couple of car-bombs I can hardly force myself to walk past a parked car.

The city was under attack for almost exactly two months, but the weight of fire poured in varied from day to day; when I look through my notes from the time I see that I once wrote that the Israeli attempts to get into the city were like the efforts of a madman trying to smash down the door of a house with an axe. He flails away in a crazed frenzy, then he tires and his battering slackens; but then the rage grips him again and he hacks away with greater vigour. That's pretty well how the Israelis did it: they would launch an utterly ferocious attack that would blanket the whole city in fire and smoke and there would be no attempt to discriminate between Palestinian or Lebanese areas, between obvious military targets like the Syrian army bunkers on the seafront near the British Embassy and obvious civilian areas like the small shopping streets around Hamra. Attacks like those were clearly meant to terrify people to the point where they wanted to surrender; they started before first light and went on until after sunset without any let-up. Then everything would be quiet, and the next couple of days would be calm as the besiegers waited to see if our nerve had cracked. Then they would be at it again, howling and screaming and battering away like demented creatures. Someone asked me later if I was scared all the time in Beirut; I said that you can't be scared all the time, any more than you can have an erection all the time because you run out of fear hormones just as you run out of sex hormones. Looking back, there were days when I actually felt very good, proud and excited that I had the nerve to stay inside the city and not run and there were others when I was so scared I literally shuddered with fear, something which until then I had thought was a reaction that existed only in the minds of thriller writers.

There were three especially bad days (in this context, a bad day was one when you couldn't convince yourself that you would be alive at the end of it). The fire came from land, sea and air and every street led to Samarra; no matter where you travelled, you would see fresh craters and shell scars on the road and you would start to wonder whether the extra glass of orange juice you had had at breakfast was what stopped you being right under the shell that had left the gaping hole in the bitumen in front of you. Those were the days when you had to make a decision at every road junction about whether to go right or left. It didn't matter, because with random fire you were as likely to be hit going in either direction, but you stopped and thought because you wanted somehow to believe you were able to exert some sort of control over your destiny. I lived in Beirut for three years and passed down several streets almost every day, and I can't describe them now; yet there are streets I used only once or twice during the siege and I remember virtually every doorway because I knew that my life might depend on being able to find a bolt-hole in the second or two after I heard the planes overhead.

The worst days were Sunday, 1 August, Wednesday, 4 August, and Thursday 12 August, and if I had to give prizes to the Israeli army, then the Ariel Sharon Prize for Sheer Mindless Savagery would probably go to the whole of the Israeli High Command for 12 August. This was the last of the three major assaults on the city, and by then I had pretty well run out of new ways of describing what was going on. On 1 and 4 August, I had run through 'shock' and 'terror' and 'mindless brutality' and 'worst since World War II' and most other ways of describing what they were trying to do to us, so that by the time I got to Thursday I had to begin by saying, 'Watching the Israeli air force smashing Beirut to pieces yesterday was like having to stand and watch a man slowly beat a sick dog to death with an axe handle.' I remember looking at that line at the time and thinking I was laying it on a bit thick – real old Fleet Street horse-shit of the 'I watched in horror today as bullets stitched a delicate tracery in the age-old palace of the emperor and an empire collapsed around me' school of British pop journalism. But looking back on it, it's not a bad simile, because Beirut was as defenceless against air attack as any sick animal is to attack by a sadist, and the Israelis were quite simply intent on brutalizing the place. This was the last major attack of the war, and there was virtually no attempt at movement on the ground. The barrage came in from the safety of the sea and the hills and the shells landed anywhere. In retrospect it was clear that Sharon's kids were not pursuing any military objective; they were simply punishing west Beirut for not giving in. I suspect that nobody will ever produce any exact casualty figures for the war because of the chaos that reigned in west Beirut as the civilian services disappeared, but I see in my notes we reporters estimated that the Israelis must have killed or badly injured 500 people that day, mostly civilians, and the majority of them women and children. There is nothing unusual about those figures. The area being blanketed with fire was very small; people had nowhere to hide because there were very few shelters, and it is a simple fact of urban warfare that civilians suffer most because they are not physically or mentally prepared – or well trained enough – to cope with war in the way that fighting men are.

This was the day when the Lebanese Prime Minister Shaik Wazzan broke off his talks with the Israelis and Philip Habib, because he finally became convinced that the Israelis were going to destroy Beirut and that the talks were Begin's way of prolonging the bombing long enough to turn west Beirut into rubble. Wazzan is a solid middle-class Lebanese lawyer of no great charisma or high-level political experience who had more or less had

the prime minister's job thrust on him after his predecessor had gone back to banking. In the normal run of things, being prime minister is no great shakes because the president is far and away the most powerful person in the country – as he is in France, which gave Lebanon her system of government. But Wazzan, a thickset, greying and politically conservative Muslim, became important because he was involved in the talks Habib was having to try and get the war ended and the P.L.O. out of Beirut. When Israel went collectively mad on 12 August, Wazzan had had enough. He called off the talks in a rage and went on the radio and told the people there was no point in talking 'because Israel is determined to wipe out the Lebanese capital anyway . . . I have told Philip Habib that I cannot carry on these talks while thousands of tons of explosives are wreaking mass destruction on my city, my capital. I didn't break up the talks but I told him I wouldn't carry on, and I also told him I hold him and the United States responsible for the consequences.

'We had talks today, but they were not about Israel's new conditions [for the P.L.O. withdrawal]. We only discussed these concentrated air-raids which have no parallels in past or present. If the Israelis want to kill us all, let them do it and have it over and done with. Let the world shoulder the responsibility for allowing this mass-acre, and let the United States accept this responsibility in the face of the rest of the world.' Wazzan stayed in Beirut for most of the war and made his name as a brave and fearless leader, so much so that when Bashir Gemayel was later elected president, he asked Wazzan to stay on, and after Bashir was killed Wazzan was retained by the new president Amin Gemayel, even though the Gemayels and Wazzan had been on opposite sides during the siege. But Wazzan was deeply scarred by the siege, and this shows in the negotiations going on in 1983 between the Lebanese and the Israelis about an Israeli pull-out. The Israelis want bases in Lebanon to consolidate their rule and Wazzan, who has lived under Israeli attack, is fighting hard against them. For this reason the Israelis are (at the end of January 1983) mounting a ferocious propaganda campaign against him as the main obstacle to 'peace'. The *Guardian* quotes an Israeli negotiator as saying Wazzan 'bears heavy responsibility for the slow movement of the talks. He is consistently and continuously blocking every move to go forwards.'

Wazzan just doesn't trust the Israelis, and neither could anyone else who had lived through 12 August, which was one of the largest terrorist attacks ever launched. I say 'terrorist attack' because it had no other purpose. When the Israelis were making a serious attempt to break through the defences, they would try to come in on the ground and the attack would have a recognizable pattern. On a day like 1 August, the day of a big push, they opened up around midnight, lighting the sky with flares and then putting a very heavy barrage

A present from Arik

into the weak points in the perimeter at the Museum Crossing, the port area and down near the airport. When this fire had pushed the defenders under cover, the tanks and A.P.C.s were cranked up and began to try to move in through these points. These were classical ground attacks and everything was well under way before first light, so that the army could use darkness as a cover. We all knew it was going to be different on 12 August – and very nasty – because the shit didn't hit until after first light, when it was too late for troop movements. I was asleep until 6.30 a.m. and for once it was not the sound of exploding shells that catapulted me out of bed but the scream of the jets overhead. I didn't leap into my nice blue New Balance running shoes thinking, 'This is a pure

sudden dive is as sharp and lethal. As they move around over Beirut, the planes eject strings of flares to distract heat-seeking missiles, so that soon the sky becomes patterned with the flashes of the flares, the puffs of white smoke they leave behind and the longer trails of white vapour left by the expiring missiles. The pilots play in this sky full of white morse dots and dashes, swooping in over the Commodore whose roof is packed with television cameras, waggling their wings or rolling over us as they finish their bombing runs – it reminded me of the way dogs race around waving their tails after a good shit. They were at it all day over the city, and it was an interesting experience for a war follower like myself because although I'd seen plenty of air-raids on guerrilla

Commodore Hotel rooftop

terrorist attack,' but the idea grew as the morning went on and the jets and ships and artillery worked us over without the hordes on the ground making any attempt to come in and get us.

They're very elegant, those Mirages and F-16s and Daggers. They fly very high to avoid the anti-aircraft fire from the Palestinians' old hand-cranked anti-aircraft guns and their shoulder-fired Sam-7 missiles (which are terrific against helicopters but fall about 10,000 feet short of jet fighter-bombers). The planes circle slowly like sharks around a dying whale, then wheel at the last minute and dive on the targets. The shark simile looks corny but it happens to be very accurate, because the bellies of the planes are silvery like a shark's and the

bunkers and forest hideaways before, I'd never seen a big city having the shit beaten out of it in an air attack. It was real World War II stuff, just get in over the target area and let 'er go. Nobody knew exactly where it was all going to hit, but by Christ somebody down there was going to feel bad by the end of the day.

If you watched a bombing raid in Vietnam or Cambodia, you didn't see all that much unless it was napalm, when you got a great red flash followed by a huge cloud of oily black smoke. In the jungle or in the rice-paddies you saw the plane dive, then the cloud of dust and smoke rise, and then the flat bang would reach you and the shock-wave would pound your eardrums . . . No big deal, and mostly in those days there would be

one sortie by three planes and the whole thing would be over in ten minutes.

But if I'd been an American taxpayer in Beirut I would have felt that I had really got my money's worth. I would have been watching my bombers dropping my bombs, courtesy of the Israeli air force, and the grand show they put on. The planes came over in waves; at one point we all went up to the top of the twelve-storey concrete skeleton of a half-built hotel on the seafront of a suburb called Raouche to watch the bombing of a whole sweep of seaside suburbs: Ramlet el Baida, Jnah, Bir Hassan. Just getting there was an unnerving experience because during the raids all forms of life would disappear from the city. In the raid you drove through almost totally deserted streets, past shuttered shops, the only movement coming from torn curtains and shredded venetian blinds flapping from broken windows. Very occasionally you would see a careering ambulance, its siren screaming, or a Palestinian jeep with a crewman in the back clinging on to his supremely ineffective 80-calibre anti-aircraft gun – the things were mounted in the back and the gunner, his legs spread apart, clung on to the handles that moved the barrel – we used to call them water-skiers because of the stance. These were brilliant summer days, perfect for the planes, and as you drove around Beirut you were half blinded by the sun glittering off the broken glass that covered the roadway.

Occasionally a 1,000-lb. bomb would drop near us – by 'near', I mean within five hundred yards. The impact was so enormous that whole buildings within that sort of radius would actually shiver; I remember watching the whole side of a glass-fronted building near the Commodore flapping like a sheet of tinfoil in the breeze. A single hit could demolish a skyscraper and often did – if the bomb broke the central steel and concrete spine of a modern building, then the rubbishy fibrecement walls and glass exteriors would simply fold up and collapse in a pile of rubble. More solid buildings would remain standing, but the concussion was so great that every window would blow in (if the bomb fell outside) or outwards, if the bomb penetrated. I was looking at the Algerian Embassy after the beachfront bombing raids, and after a while it occurred to me that it looked exactly as if someone had pumped it up like a balloon and then popped it – it had just burst outwards, although the main walls still stood. From our twelfth-floor grandstand the bombing was exciting to watch; there can be no other way of describing the pure spectacle of destruction. Out on the shining bay to our right were the gunboats pumping in shells; above us in the brilliant blue sky were the tiny dots of the planes diving in; and below us to the left, a mile of seafront was disappearing under tons of best high-grade American explosive. Their flat trajectory meant the navy guns usually hit a building, so that with them firing you would see flashes of flame and through binoculars, bits of concrete and wood and metalwork flying into the air. Diving steeply, the planes would quite

often miss, and the bombs would dig deep into the soft red earth before exploding and throwing giant clouds of red dust and explosive fumes into the air. Occasionally someone would throw in a few white phosphorus shells so that at the peak of an attack the whole seafront would be a curtain of fire, red dust and white smoke, boiling upwards in what I thought of at the time as the Beirut version of a firestorm. We were at one end of the curve of a bay, and this great panorama of destruction was therefore a strip of violent reds and whites painted on a backdrop of blue sky and water. It was simply a grand and terrible spectacle; seen across the water, it was pretty much like watching a war movie on a big screen with sensurround, or whatever that system is that rocks your seat and makes the walls quiver with the power of the amplification system. Twelve storeys in the air and a mile away, you felt as divorced from the reality of what you saw as if you were at the movies. Get closer than that, like within a hundred yards, and it isn't anywhere near as grand and exciting – you're more likely to shit yourself than shiver with excitement.

I suppose the closest I came to being killed, all the time I was in Beirut, was in a rocket attack where the first one exploded no more than fifteen yards away from the photographer Don McCullin and I as we were being driven to the office along Rue Souraty, a small shopping street parallel to Hamra. If I ever do get blown away, it will probably be by the sort of thing that nearly got us that time. I won't be doing anything gallant like running through no-man's-land to rescue a friend, or going across some border in the leading tank. I'll be squatting behind a bush or having breakfast by the swimming pool and some stray round will knock a flower-pot off the balcony and it will fall on my head.

The attack that caught us came in that category; it was an otherwise quiet day, we were in a civilian shopping street that had never been hit and we were going to the office to send a telex saying that we were all okay. Meanwhile however, down in Beirut's battered port area, Sergeant Weinberger or whoever was lighting the blue touchpaper on the Stalin Organ rocket-launcher that he and his friends had captured from the Palestinians in south Lebanon and driven up to Beirut to demonstrate.

The trouble with rockets (if you're on the wrong end of an attack) is that they're very sudden and very random. The first hit the roadway about forty feet away and I distinctly remember seeing a big red flash, a novelty because I'd never been close enough for that before. The driver stopped the car but we were paralysed – not by fear, because it was too sudden, just bereft of movement – and we sat there while the next one smashed through the window of an apartment two floors above us. We were out of the car and running for a doorway when the third landed in the roadway and the shrapnel whined past us; the fourth took out a huge crumbly section of stone wall in an old apartment block a

28

Ouzai

hundred yards ahead of us at a T-intersection. By now we were in the foyer of an apartment and quite safe; the fragments were whizzing past the open door, and we were relaxed enough to listen for the whistle of the rockets before they fell. You heard a brief whining sound, then a tremendous crash as the thing burst through a wall and exploded, then there was the sound of a cascade of broken glass hitting the road, followed by a brief but complete silence. Then the screaming began in the burst-open apartments above us; a minute later, the first people started running out into the street, some rushing blindly for the nearest doorway, others scream-ing hysterically and pointing to the craters up above them. Several of the men were in pyjamas because it was afternoon and siesta-time, and a man in striped pyjamas ran past me, carrying a crying child in one hand and dragging another one covered in blood and with its feet dragging through the broken glass. Most people who ran into the street were bleeding from broken-glass slashes but the fact that they were able to move meant they were still only slightly hurt. The seriously injured were the ones still screaming from the upper floors; you could see people trembling in the doorways, agonizing whether to stay in safety or risk running across the street to try and help the wounded. The first salvo probably had about five rockets in it and there was a similar one about two minutes later, when we were just beginning to think the

attack was over. What sticks in my mind is that this was only a middle-class Lebanese commercial street, lined with what had once been expensive dress shops, and with family apartments above them. I used it all the time because it was a quick route to the office, and I don't think I ever saw a military vehicle in it, other than the jeeps which ran everywhere. It was certainly true that on that day the only people hurt were Lebanese although oddly enough, there was a P.L.O. loss. A Fateh officer had parked a jeep around the corner from where we were, and when the area quietened down we saw a piece of concrete had been chipped off a balcony and bent his Kalashnikov into a horseshoe shape. I counted at least ten Lebanese wounded; I was told, although I did not see the bodies, that two women had been killed in an upstairs apartment when the rocket exploded in their living-room.

The civilians were the people who suffered most. I used to post a photographer outside the biggest and best-equipped hospital in west Beirut, the American University Hospital just off Hamra, simply to record the events of the day as the ambulances shuttled backwards and forwards between the areas being bombarded and the emergency department. He would come back with a different catalogue of horrors every day: the child whose leg still smoked when they took the bandages off and found the phosphorus burning its way to the bone underneath; the woman caught side-on by some sort of incendiary blast that had charred all the left side of her face and left her eye shrivelled in its socket like a fried oyster; the twitching thing rolled up in a blood-soaked blanket that they had unrolled as Jan Morvan watched. 'What,' said Jan, who is French, 'is the English word for *pâté*?'

Catherine photographed a family in the exclusively Lebanese suburb of Basta where the city's antique shops are concentrated. They lived in a tiny makeshift apartment built on the flat roof of an eleven-storey building, and the shell crashed into the children's bedroom in the middle of the night. Her mother found her daughter

used. We had to bundle his body in plastic sheets; but when we drove towards the cemetery, it was being shelled and we had to turn back. We had to dig a grave in the garden.'

How many horror stories can you tell before people grow tired of them? In a way I suppose, horror was commonplace; what was more extraordinary was that people still tried to live normal lives, despite the bombardment. Beirut's best newspaper *An Nahar*, was published virtually every day, and its editor François Akl told me that one of the proofs of the paper's continuing independence was that the staff refused to move to the safety of east Beirut to produce it: 'I'm not going

Lina Assaf and family

Lina Assaf, who is eleven, lying with the blood fountaining out of the stump where her left leg used to be. Beside her drenched in blood, was her seven-year-old sister Linda screaming in hysterical fear. As her mother said, the blood washed Linda's mind away; she remains a mental cripple to this day. In one of my own notebooks I find I have recorded a story told me by Patrick Smith, whose family owns a famous grocery store in west Beirut. He was talking about the death of his friend, Karim. 'We wanted to bury him, but we couldn't find a coffin in the whole of west Beirut – they had all been

to be pushed around by Israeli gunners,' he told me as we sat enjoying the breeze in his office. The breeze was there because all the windows had been blown out by shelling and about ten feet from his office was a giant hole that had been created by a direct hit on the wall of the next-door building. The Israelis did stop *An Nahar* temporarily by shelling it closed and the staff believe it was hit deliberately to stop it publishing the issue that would have commemorated its fiftieth anniversary. The gunners had a good result against the press that day: they not only knocked out *An Nahar*, but *Newsweek* and

United Press International as well. We were in the same building as *An Nahar* and a single 155-mm. phosphorus shell smashed into the fifth floor, obliterated our office as it exploded through our ceiling, and still had enough momentum to burst through our door and into U.P.I. where it burned out their main office. I was out in the street at that time, trying to get Don McCullin between me and the rockets that suddenly blanketed us. The same rocket attack drove the journalists in the offices of *An Nahar* down to the basement, and the phosphorus shell arrived about five minutes later. A week later I brushed against the great red phosphorus splash that decorated the office wall like a Morris Louis painting – and my arm was still burning gently an hour later . . . You don't let yourself think about what it would have been like if you'd been there when the thing hit.

When I think how dangerous it was just to be in west Beirut, I'm amazed at how many people, who could have left, not only stayed but tried to live normal lives. Most days, you could go to the Myrtom House Restaurant where the Austrian owner Hans Matchek, in between moaning about how the staff had deserted, would cook a *Wiener Schnitzel* and find a cold bottle of *Gewürtztraminer*. Before it was finally blown away, I could walk round the corner from my office and buy a hot cheese sandwich; down the road, Middle East Airlines were always open and taking bookings, even though the airport was under constant fire and five of their planes were burnt out on the runway. The bookings were mainly for a handful of flights they were operating outside Beirut, but if you were an optimist you could book your flight to Europe for Christmas. My optician, an Armenian who was the Harry of Harry's Optic on Abdel Aziz Street, closed only at those times when the Israelis appeared to be rehearsing for the Third World War, and he made me a new pair of specs after I smashed one set hitting the road in a hurry in Fakhani.

Through it all, my personal historical adviser Professor Kamal Salibi worked on a line of research at the American University which if successful will change history as we know it, or at least give Menachem Begin an excuse to add Saudi Arabia and South Yemen to Eretz Israel. I have all my notes here; but I have a feeling I'm now going to get this wrong, although it is easy to outline what Kamal was doing.

Essentially he had decided that early interpreters of the Bible had misread place-names, and that many of the events in the Old Testament couldn't have taken place in the biblical area of Israel and Jordan but had happened much further south, in South Yemen and western Saudi Arabia.

That's the easy bit, and I probably would be able to explain what follows more clearly if there hadn't been a war going on outside at the time, something Kamal had apparently not noticed. The gunboats were banging away in the harbour stretched out below us, and Kamal was telling me about a place called Hazarmaveth which

is a place-name that first appears in the Bible in Genesis (10:26). It cropped up originally when in his role as a semitic scholar, Kamal was studying place-names in southern Arabia to see if they would give any indication as to the language spoken by the original inhabitants. He came across an oasis called Hadramut and was struck by the name's similarity to Hazarmaveth. The two don't look that much alike in English but written in Hebrew or Arabic which have no vowels, the two are close together. He concluded that what had happened is that the Mazoretes, the Jewish scholars who had edited and added the vowels of the ancient Hebrew scriptures between the sixth and ninth centuries, had put in the wrong vowels. Hazarmaveth means 'abode of death' in Hebrew but, try as he could, he couldn't find such a place in the biblical land of Canaan. 'But Hadramut could come from a root meaning "green" or "to dwell", and I know Hadramut is one of the greenest oases in southern Arabia, because I've been there.' Beginning with Hadramut, he checked out a whole series of south Arabian and Yemeni place-names against biblical names, especially those with topographical descriptions. 'To my astonishment, I found a whole series of Arabian place-names which coincide with names in the Bible and which fit topographical descriptions: place A which is fifteen miles west of place B in the Bible is the same distance and direction from place B in Saudi Arabia. But if you look where biblical scholars have tried to put them within the accepted biblical lands, it is clear they are just guessing. Essentially, my research seems to indicate that all the books of the Bible from Genesis to Malachi were written in or about Arabia.' Kamal's overall conclusion is that the people who are the progenitors of Menachem Begin and Yasser Arafat probably once belonged to a single tribe in Arabia who split in two, with one half going to the oases of southern Arabia and the other half north to the lands of the Bible.

They were all out of their minds, the Lebanese and the foreigners who stayed in Beirut. Every day brought a new way of dying, and yet they wouldn't leave and of course thousands of them were killed or wounded. I have the greatest respect for them because by being there they gave Beirut a stability it would have lost if the only people left had been the fighters and Palestinian civilians. Solid citizens – like Harry the optician and the staff of M.E.A. in their uniforms and the dozens of European doctors and nurses and welfare workers reassured others by their presence: if they were there, it couldn't be all that bad. In reality it was very very bad indeed, not only because of the intensity of the bombardments, but because of the length of the siege. I have been in more dangerous places for short spells of time, but I've never had to wake up every day for something like six weeks knowing that if I got unlucky I was going to be in terrible trouble.

But life for me was much easier than for most of the people caught in the city. I could eat three times a day and shower in (admittedly, red salty) water; I had a comfortable room with electricity for several hours a day, and I was being paid and getting by-lines for being in a place I felt I had to be. Life was harder for almost everyone else and very, very short on glory, comfort or money. I once asked Kamal Salibi why he stayed when he could have taken his documents and worked safely on the other side of the city; he said, 'There are times when I think we need a rest, that we deserve a rest because we've given more than enough support to another people's revolution. Then I ask myself whether we should cease to support a revolution that is a genuine one, whether we should close our borders and reduce Lebanon to an insignificant little nation of 10,000 square kilometres. Should we become a banana republic under Israeli sponsorship? If you think it through, you have no choice but to prove your independence by staying.'

Two days later, I returned to the American University to talk to a group of women who had been goaded to the pitch of marching through the perimeter to protest to the Israelis about their tactic of trying to starve people out. Among them were doctors and nurses and some foreign medical people, but a number were Lebanese women of all religions and incomes who were enraged enough by what was being done to them and to their city to

actually risk their lives to make a debating point. They were sitting under the trees in the University campus, waiting in the shade of an old yellowstone faculty building for their friends to come and join them in a march through the no-man's-land of the crossing-point known as Galerie Semaan, named after a big store which once dominated the road and was then just a ruin. I ran around taking notes, although I knew at the time that their little protest would never make a thirty-second story on television or six paragraphs in a newspaper – unless, of course, the Israelis or the Phalangists opened up and blew them away as they marched on the crossing. Every day in Beirut in those days there was a disaster of such titanic proportions that no women's march could make it into the news. The women were all sitting around, talking about what the shortages were doing to the hospitals and how they were getting their first cases of kids dying from dehydration. I remember a woman called Adila Labban whose husband was of all things, the Minister of Social Services in Lebanon; she was talking about how Kol Israel (the Israeli radio) had just proudly announced that after weeks of blockade, supplies of food were generously being allowed into the city that day by a magnanimous Israeli army. 'What they didn't say was that they were still keeping the water

The flies ate first

supply cut – how do they think people are going to make bread without water – or do they expect us to eat handfuls of dry flour?'

They were a curiously mixed group of people. There was a group of Scandinavian nurses – the kind who get pilloried in right-wing papers because they always seem to rally to left-wing or rebel causes – never mind that most of the 'rebels' are injured women and kids. With them were very straight Lebanese matrons who were outraged that a pack of foreigners were preventing them from living their own lives in their own cities, women like Daad Rubeiz, a slim and elegant Lebanese doctor who I suspect had been a prop of middle-class Beirut society before Operation Peace For Galilee turned her around. I think she was probably more furious with the Americans who had supplied the Israeli army than with the Israelis themselves. 'We all used to be so pro-American here, this country was the most pro-American in the Middle East. Now, every day, people like me become more anti-American.' She was totally convinced that the siege of Beirut had nothing to do with getting rid of the Palestinians. 'The Israelis came here to add Lebanon to their empire. Even if we get some sort of a peaceful settlement here, they won't leave. They'll be here for years to come.' So far she has not been proved wrong. She mused on why she was talking like this to a reporter who was writing it all down. 'Do you know I didn't really have an identity of my own before this war; I was never really affirmative about anything. Now I've been close to death so many times that I feel I have to say and do something, because I don't know if I'll be here tomorrow.'

The women's march was one of the more bizarre events of the siege. We drove in a long convoy of press cars behind two small buses carrying the women, at last reaching the huge piled-up earth barriers the defenders had thrown up as anti-tank defences. Once past these earth heaps, the road to east Beirut stretched ahead of us, rising quite steeply up the hill to the Christian suburb of Hazmiyeh. The actual Israeli/Phalangist checkpoint was probably 300 yards away, halfway up the rise – and all that way without any cover at all. The buildings are set a long way back from the road at that point; we went down the centre, the group of about thirty women in the middle and the flock of reporters orbiting around them. The women knew what they were doing, but I was not so sure why I was there. It occurred to me that we were very exposed, and that by this time so many atrocities had been committed that another one caused by some trigger-happy sniper opening up, wouldn't bother any

The day the besiegers broke their drought

33

combatants overmuch. I had an itchy feeling in my back and my front, and I was only distracted by an Australian named Jean Calder walking with me. She had come to Lebanon because 1981 was the Year of the Disabled, and she, a physiotherapist who specialized in treating disabled children, had heard that Lebanon had plenty of raw material. She had been working in Palestinian hospitals and had been bombed in and out of hospitals around Beirut like the target in a T.V. video game, dragging her contingent of crippled kids with her. She had become a surrogate mother to a six-year-old blind girl who had been found wandering in the wreckage of Tyre, and to an eight-year-old spastic quadriplegic boy whose family had all been killed in Tal Zaatar (that name crops up again and again in any story about Beirut Palestinians). 'The kids are all terrified of the sound of planes, any planes. They associate the sound with bombing. My little girl keeps saying "I want to hit them". It's very hard to explain to kids that someone is trying to kill them, but we've now moved five times and so they realize that perhaps someone is chasing them. Last week we were caught in the open in a bombing attack and I found myself running with the blind girl under one arm and the quadriplegic under the other, and wondering where I should be running. You know, one of the things they don't teach you when you're doing your doctorate is what to do when you get caught in a bombing attack and you're taking a group of crippled kids out in the fresh air in their wheelchairs. It's hard to believe that this is 1982 and the world is just letting this happen.'

We were now approaching the rolls of barbed wire that the Phalangists had stretched across the road to close their checkpoint. If we had already been an exotic group at the beginning, we were more of one now. Our leader was an aristocratic Englishwoman and walking in our midst was a very beautiful white horse. The Englishwoman was Pamela Cooper, a very tall and commanding woman whose son the Earl of Gowrie is a minister in the Thatcher government. She was in Beirut with her second husband Major John Cooper, and both of them were working for the Red Cross. The white horse belonged to a millionaire racehorse-owner; it had been trapped on our side in its stable near the green line when the siege began. The owner wanted it taken to safety in the east, but the leftist militiamen had seen that it was clearly a piece of capitalist property and refused to let the groom take it through the west-side crossing. The man had waited patiently while people crossed in a thin trickle, and when our milling crew of women protesters, drivers, reporters and television technicians descended on the line, he simply manoeuvred the horse into our midst and marched with us. When we finally got to the barbed wire, man and horse were given immediate entry, while the women were stopped dead by a completely hysterical Phalangist officer in a brand-new green uniform, waving his pistol in the air and shouting, 'What you want, what you want? Not any pictures, not any pictures.'

'We come from every nation,' said Pamela Cooper through a small hand-held loudspeaker. (Not quite accurate, but I had counted women of a dozen nationalities.) 'We come to protest. Beirut is not a testing-ground for sophisticated weapons. Stop bombing Beirut.' The not-any-pictures man was working himself into a frenzy, demanding that we leave immediately and Pamela Cooper didn't do his self-esteem any good by totally ignoring him and asking to see the person in charge. 'I want to see an Israeli officer,' she said in the sort of tone I could see her using back home to summon the manager at Harrods. Eventually one of the guards scurried back up the hill to look for the officer; while we waited, various Israeli soldiers and an Israeli television crew pushed their way through the Phalangist line and came up to the wire to take in the show. 'We have witnessed the killing and maiming of large numbers of civilians by cluster-bombs and phosphorus shells,' Pamela Cooper told them. 'Two-thirds of the casualties are civilians. There is a terrible shortage of food, medicine and water.' As she spoke, an Israeli major came slowly down the hill, speaking quietly in English to a Lebanese officer. He was probably a reservist, he carried the waist-line of a middle-aged insurance manager bulging over his army belt; he made no attempt to approach the women, but stood in the background behind his own men. The women were now taking turns to deliver their messages in their own languages.

Among the languages I heard were Norwegian, French, Dutch, Swedish, Chinese, Japanese, Arabic, English and Tagalog. They were mostly either appeals for help or pleas to stop the bombing, most of which I understood only vaguely. A nurse with a strong New Zealand accent shouted across the wire, 'If we don't get medicine now, people are going to start dying of cholera and typhoid, and the children will die first.' How much of it was understood I don't know, and it's a pity we didn't have a Hebrew speaker; but the officer would have heard the English and I am fairly sure that at least a couple of the soldiers spoke Arabic. It was all academic, because none of them had any interest in what was being said. They stood as if held by that dumb curiosity that brings sheep and cows to a fence in a country lane when you stop to look over the wire. There was enough action going on to move them close to us but not enough to prompt them into any further action. They had the same lack of concern for what the women were doing as the soldiers had on the road to Sofar when the travellers were begging to be allowed to cross through the wire. We could all have been animals behind the wire at Whipsnade: amusing, almost human in the way we were behaving, and worth a two-minute stop before lunch. Two minutes was about what the women got, then the Israelis turned away and the women wound their cotton banners, lettered with the messages they had just shouted, through the strands of barbed wire before going back the way we had all come. They had made no impression at all on our besiegers.

This happened on 10 August, and I was back at the hotel in time for the two o'clock Radio Israel news – 'the voice of the beast', as everyone called it. I scribbled some notes about the broadcast and on one page wrote, 'The roar of the bombers overhead made it almost impossible to hear the radio saying that Beirut is quiet today.' The same broadcast quoted Begin raging about an attack on a Jewish restaurant in Paris. He invoked the shades of the Dreyfus case and apparently intended to call on French-Jewish youth to rise to protect themselves. Someone looked up at the jet-trails in the sky and joked that maybe Begin would divert a few of the Skyhawks and put a strike into the Elysée Palace . . . Could never have happened, of course. Not that we knew it at the time, but all those jets were going to be needed two days later when the final attempt to smash Beirut, 'Horrendous Thursday', was launched.

When I returned to Beirut in November, there were two Thai bar-girls in the Cloud Nine Bar across the road from the Commodore, and the rubble had gone from the streets. They had cleared the street-traders off the footpaths of Hamra, the shops had new plate-glass and the first Christmas decorations were appearing among the goodies. In the street where McCullin and I had cowered under the rocket attack, a dress shop called Carel had reopened with a window display that had as its centrepiece a short, flame-red evening dress priced at £600. At Ted Lapidus, just up the road from my office,

you could buy a pair of pale grey shoes to go with your pale grey silk suit, and in the Concorde cinema complex where I had last seen 400 Palestinian refugees from Damour camping out in the corridors, I saw that Yves St Laurent had reopened and was offering among other articles, a red leather knickerbocker suit for £800. The ruins of a building in Rue Assi, where Catherine had photographed watchers waiting for bodies to be dug out, had simply disappeared; all that remained was an area of fresh earth that might have been somebody's vegetable patch.

There was a time when I might have jumped up and down at this sudden show of wealth and started asking heated questions about how people could flaunt their wealth while refugees were starving in the camps. I have nothing but contempt for the chickenshit diplomats who left their embassies in west Beirut to operate in comfort in the east during the war, and I feel the same for the carpetbaggers who sat out the siege in Paris and London. But poor old west Beirut needs a clean-up and red leather knickerbocker suits are a sign of the return of a sort of normalcy. My experience is that Beirut rarely stays normal for long; but while things are quiet, I think people, especially those who would not be booted out, deserve clean streets and bright shop-windows and pretty clothes and open bars. They are, after all, a select group of individuals, people who each have a story which begins: 'I just missed being killed on the day . . .'

3
'Nobody Cares'

They were waiting for me when I got back home in the middle of the afternoon. It was something I never did normally; I usually went off to the Lamb House for *shish taouk* and salad and *arak* and talk, sitting there half the afternoon picking at garlicky chicken, filling and refilling the *arak* glasses, solving the Lebanese war. Then back to the office to look at the cables before going back to the Commodore for the evening's festivities . . . all this, of course, in the good old days when you could live safely in a house because it was during the middle of the civil war and the Phalangists didn't have anything much bigger than heavy machine-guns and mortars, and my house was safe from them because it was on the far side of the American University staff quarters, so that the academics would get it, rather than the *Newsweek* man on the spot. I walked home early that day because I had forgotten my passport and had been told without warning that I was getting an Iraqi visa.

I took the scenic route home, past the American University on Rue Bliss, then down the long flight of steps leading to my house at the bottom of the hill. Fifty yards beyond the bottom step was my house, one of the last old Arab houses in a section now covered with concrete blocks of the University staff quarters, the British Embassy on the seafront and a hundred yards further back, the American school, once the biggest American school in the Middle East but then almost deserted, peopled by half a dozen teachers and the hundred or so children of the last Americans left in Beirut.

If I'd been the ace reporter I always think myself to be, I probably would have noticed the teenage kid leaning against the stone wall of the staff quarters – but there were always teenage kids around in those days, there were few schools and no jobs, and so there were kids

everywhere. Anyway, my house was totally secure: it had more gates than the average medieval castle and all the windows had iron bars on them. I opened the steel front gate, locked it behind me, opened the wrought-iron inner gate, locked it behind me, walked across the inner patio, opened the wooden door to the living-room – and had it closed behind me by the kid with the ·38 stuck in my back. I probably wouldn't have struggled at all, but the second man grabbed me and I tried to pull away and turn back to get out. It was easy enough to break away because I was greasy with sweat from fear and he was equally sweaty, maybe from fear, maybe excitement. As we struggled, it was dawning on me that I hadn't locked the bad guys out, I had locked them in with me: the third one, the one who had been leaning on the wall outside, was now coming through the back window where the bars had been sawn through and pulled open. The thought that I had locked myself in was followed by two conflicting ideas: if I struggled I might only annoy them to the point where they would shoot me to stop me jumping around; on the other hand, if I just stood there and did nothing and let them tie me up with the rope the third one was now waving, I would be utterly helpless and if they decided to shoot me I would go down like a sheep in a slaughterhouse. One thing was for sure: if they were going to shoot me, it would be easy for them because there was no law and order in Beirut, hadn't been for years. This town had been a city of anonymous corpses since 1975 and one more wouldn't make any difference; nobody would tell the police because what was left of the police wouldn't do anything, and anyway this was an isolated house with clearly only one person in it. In the end I let them tie me up. I had no chance of knocking out one – let alone three; I couldn't get out of the place, and they were starting to shout at me in Arabic: I didn't understand a word, but it wasn't friendly. They lay me on the cold tiled floor, tied my hands behind my back then my feet to my hands, and there I was, belly down, face turned to the side, pressed against the records they had piled up to take away. I clearly recall the one in front of the stack was 'Way out West' by Sonny Rollins, with the great man looking ludicrous in cowboy gear and a stetson posed out in the desert somewhere. Then the tallest of the kids, one with a fluffy brown afro, stuck his revolver in my ear and said, 'Now you die.'

In Gerry Seymour's book *Harry's Game*, which is about Northern Ireland, some gunmen are talking about putting a hood over a man before they shoot him, and how he started to piss himself when he knew he was going to get it. I didn't have any thoughts or feelings at all, just the sort of feeling of time suspended you get when you jump or dive into water from a high board or bridge . . . weightlessness, suspension of now in anticipation of the impact to come. Then they were laughing and telling me I was a coward because I tensed myself up, and then they said, 'Thank you, mister,' and went off with Sonny Rollins and the record-player.

'I thought you might be having trouble in there,' said the gatekeeper of the American University across the road when I humped my well-trussed way out like a caterpillar on a cabbage leaf. 'I saw them going in there and didn't see them come out, so I thought they might be robbing the place.'

Only later do you think about what happens when the man with the gun doesn't laugh but pulls the trigger instead. Amazing how much blood comes out of a head-shot: your brain doesn't control your heart so even when your brain is all over the ground, your heart just keeps pumping away, shoving the stuff out until the whole couple of gallons is all around you. It was taking place in Lebanon all the time: all those people who just happened to be in the wrong place when someone did something nasty to someone who wasn't the same religion. By the end of 1976, you were very blasé about it.

I remember going to Kamal Jumblatt's funeral – he was one of the better leaders, so somebody assassinated him and he was buried by his people the Druse, just near his big old Turkish house in the mountains and near where his father was buried – he'd been assassinated too, and Jumblatt would often say he expected the same thing. The whole Chouf was going crazy: long lines of people in black clothes winding up to the house, the rain thundering down, clouds of steam rising from the walkers as their bodies heated up under the effort of picking their way up the steep muddy slopes, the boom of thunder and

Victors and vanquished, Beirut 1976

the continuous crackle of A.K.-47s. Everyone who had a gun was firing into the air, spraying it around for poor old Jumblatt and his driver and bodyguard, laid out in their coffins on the big stone courtyard.

I was desperate for a piss; we'd been driving for four hours, creeping through the lines of black-draped Druse, struggling into the red mud on the sides of the tracks, and in the final hour the Clifton bladder was throbbing with every extra bump. We'd be spending two hours watching Jumblatt being buried and you can't take a leak in the middle of a funeral – on the other hand, you can't concentrate on what's happening around you when the top of your bladder is pressing against the back of your throat. I was with some Scandinavian or other – one of those reporters for a paper with *Dag* somewhere in the title – who turn up all over the Middle East, stay a week with selfless Scandinavian volunteers looking after homeless refugees, then spend eight hours on the only telex sending off reams of stuff in one of those languages you normally only see on the labels of Akvavit bottles. I think he probably followed me because he thought I was on to some sort of hot scoop, although what he thought I was going to find among the olive trees I still cannot imagine.

I suppose I realized I was getting too used to anonymous corpses when I stumbled over a body and walked straight on for another five yards to find enough shelter from the wind to piss without it all getting blown back over my already soaking pants. The little man must have been shot in the last hour; the blood from the head-wound was puddled under his head, still not washed away by the rain. It's six years ago now, and I don't remember too much about the way he looked, except that he was small, about five feet tall, wore a sort of baggy blue pin-striped suit – ridiculous clothes for a man who could only have been a farm worker – and had a slight stubble on his chin, the sort of stubble you intend to shave off when you wake, but don't get a chance because the door has been kicked in and men with the A.K.-47s are standing round your bed, or maybe dragging you towards the door.

I never saw his house, but I can imagine what it was like: two rooms, made of local yellow stone, stove, television, table and chairs, cooking pots, farm implements against the wall in one room, doorway to the next covered by a curtain, but no door. The other room would be the bedroom, maybe with one double bed with an old pink mattress with grey stripes on it and one grey blanket. There would be a mirror on one wall and, no question, on the other some kind of Christian symbol . . . maybe a crucifix, maybe a picture of a sad-eyed Jesus with long blond hair – long blond hair, even in the Middle East. It would have been a little house on the edge of some village up there in the Chouf, too far away, especially in the rain, for the neighbours to have noticed the men with the guns arriving in (and you can bet on this, too) an old Mercedes. They would have been rounding up Christians to pay for Jumblatt's death, and the little man would have known why they were there because Jumblatt had been killed the day before and it was the only news he would have heard on the portable radio on the kitchen table.

If I'd been blown away in my house and they'd found me before the heat did terrible things to my complexion, they would have reported that I had a surprised look on my face. When you're a white man out there in the third world, you never quite believe that the natives are going to do much more than shout and jump up and down and wave their guns and maybe deport you. It's because after Europe and America everyone is so polite and so hospitable that after a while you can't believe that anyone would ever do you any real harm – so when a South Vietnamese or a Pakistani or a Palestinian soldier waves a rifle in your face you smile and maybe even walk on, pretending you don't understand Urdu or Vietnamese or Arabic. It's not something you would do to a cop in Chicago or a British soldier in Belfast – but when you're a round-eye among the little brown people, you feel that nobody's out to get you.

But the little man being washed clean by the rain that was spraying off the silvery leaves of the olive trees would have known that there was no point in smiling and pretending he didn't understand. There was no look of surprise on his face . . . resignation, maybe. I wondered if he had thought of struggling like I had, and I decided he probably hadn't. He would have realized that if he had, they would have shot him then and there; he probably hoped dimly that if he went with them, some sort of cavalry might arrive before they blew him away. They'd clearly taken him to the grove to shoot him because he wouldn't have been there by choice on a day like this; and he'd just been shot because the blood was still dribbling from around his head into the muddy stream rushing through the grove. I was still having my piss when the Swede, or whatever he was, grabbed me and started shouting about how a man was dead and we had to tell someone there had been a murder.

What do you tell a man like that? Here he's spent his life in one of those countries you could cover from end to end with those labels that say 'sanitized for your personal convenience', where they call an emergency session of parliament if there's a dead dog found in the street – and suddenly there are dead men all over the place and the police must be told. How do you explain that the man has just been shot by someone like the mad-eyed gunman now standing by your parked car and firing bursts from his A.K.-47 over your head to indicate that you should move on? You tell the man from the Arctic Circle to be quiet, not to attract attention to himself, and certainly to stop shouting about bodies in olive groves, because that sort of talk makes the locals think you are some sort of foreign trouble-maker.

I stayed for the burial, which was like something out of a German movie from the '20s, with crazed Druse gunmen screaming and firing into the air, and crowds of men literally steaming in the wet air, trampling on one another to touch the old man's coffin, and finally falling headlong into his open grave. By then I had forgotten the little man in the olive trees; he really had been banished from my memory until I settled down to write this. The Swede and myself and the dead man's family are probably the only people who remember him now; the family will still wonder where he died, because by now they will know he is dead. If you were a poet, you'd like to think that red poppies will grow where he finally melted into the ground; if you were a Beirut journalist, you'd know the place where he died was the raw patch of earth where the dogs had been scrabbling.

me asks a lot of questions, but the main one is about the splash of blood to his left. I would have said that he was probably shot by a sniper rather than executed, and that at least he held himself upright long enough for the blood to run down his chest and on to his trousers – maybe he was staggering along that neatly tiled street before falling forward on his face where that patch of blood is on the left. Then later someone came along, saw the body lying on its face and turned it over to see if it was anyone they knew . . . it obviously wasn't, because the man is still there, although the guy who turned him over probably took his guns.

This is Beirut . . . the Switzerland of the Middle East where a man can lie dead on a main street, smeared with

That little man's death was almost completely anonymous. He died watched only by the men who shot him; he was probably recognizable only long enough to register in the memory-tapes of an Australian reporter who needed a piss before he saw Kamal Jumblatt buried. Yet washed in the rain in that lonely olive grove, was his death any more anonymous than that of the man Catherine Leroy photographed near the green line where the two Beiruts met and snarled at each other? There he lies in his white rollneck sweater, with the huge splash of blood on the chest, the banana-clip A.K.-47 magazine strapped to his waist, as is a holster, although the pistol is gone. The old Melbourne inquest reporter in

his own blood, and just about manage to attract the attention of passers-by. In a sense this is the ultimate in anonymous death, because this is not a decaying or defaced corpse: this is a newly dead man, recognizable to anyone who knew him. Yet there are no local police to pick him up, no newspapers to print his picture, no television station to flash his face on the screen (there are plenty of papers and television stations, but since when have nameless bodies been news in Beirut?). For all I know, his wife and children are wondering even now what happened to Dad after he slung his A.K. over his shoulder, stuffed his ·38 in its holster and walked out to war. They'll know he's dead by now; but will they be turning over the pages of this book in Antoine's in Hamra in 1983 and realize for the first time what really happened? Chastening thought. If it had been me, would I have attracted a better sort of crowd? Dead Arabs, that's one thing: they step over them like they step over dogshit on East 58th Street or Fulham Broadway; but would those people have ignored my nice blond-haired body in my Saigon-made safari suit, with my notebook rather than an A.K. magazine stuck in my pocket? Well let's be realistic: even if I didn't get a crowd, Catherine would have had me towed back to the Australian Embassy. This guy probably got the quicklime-and-bulldozer treatment, along with the other corpses of the week.

When it's all over in Lebanon – if it ever ends in Lebanon – thousands of people will live with memories of friends or relations who were dragged away or who never came home; thousands of anonymous corpses will slowly be absorbed back into the red earth. More than anything, it is the anonymity of death that sinks into the subconscious, like those deliquescing corpses melting into the earth, and resurfaces in the memory like a skeleton in a bulldozer's shovel when you see the pictures. Suddenly I remember the corpse on the Fuad Chebab bridge between east and west Beirut, earlier in the war, before the Israelis came in on the ground. It was on the eastern side of the bridge, so it was probably a Lebanese Muslim or Palestinian of any persuasion who had struck it unlucky. He had been soaked in petrol and set alight; the flames had burnt through the neck, and somehow – it might have just been someone with a sense of humour – the loose, blackened head with only the white teeth showing had rolled, or been moved, so that it rested by the foot. That corpse was there for at least a week, because there were too many snipers around for anyone to pick the thing up. One day it was gone but nobody could ever have known who that blackened bundle had ever been, although I guess it's safe enough to write all this on the assumption it was a man. Generally speaking, people didn't go round setting women on fire: shoot them all right, maybe disembowel them, that sort of thing, but raping them or setting them on fire was generally regarded as being the sort of thing a gentleman wouldn't do. Maybe they screamed a lot when you set them on fire or they jumped up and down and were a fire hazard because they sprayed burning petrol all over the place, or they swelled up and popped, because they're put together differently inside – whatever it was, burning women wasn't high on the list of national pastimes. Really it wasn't until the Israelis came with phosphorus and incendiaries that burning women alive played much of a role in the business of population control in West Beirut. (It must be emphasized, of course, that the last sentence should not be interpreted as suggesting that the sponsors of Operation Peace For Galilee practised some sort of positive or reverse discrimination in favour of women when distributing incendiary ordnance; everyone got their share, even little kids too small to get to the front of the queue.)

The anonymous corpses from before the siege tend to stick in the mind, because for the most part they came in ones or twos. You never knew who the woman was outside Tyre in south Lebanon whose house was hit by the 500-pounder, courtesy of the Israeli air force. She was, when you saw her, just a pile of dusty meat on a stretcher; and you knew she was a woman only because the one recognizable piece of human anatomy on the pile, a solitary foot, had an anklet of red beads on it. But you remember that particular pile of meat; and the people in what remained of the village gave it a name because a third of them survived, and they knew there was only one woman in that pile of rubble who wore a red bead anklet.

Little villages are one thing – in little villages if only one survives he'll remember the others. Beirut was different. Half a million people were packed inside the perimeter. The rockets and the bombs were coming in day and night, the buildings were collapsing, cars full of people were burning so completely that even the bones turned to ash. You can dig out a small village, even when all twenty houses have been flattened and for the most part, what you drag out of the ruins will be recognizable. In Beirut, rows of buildings came down, and the little white ambulances rushed dementedly from neighbour-hood to neighbourhood carrying off the wounded, leaving the fit survivors to scrabble around in the dust and concrete and broken glass for the friends and brothers and parents and sisters they knew had to be buried. A really solid hit from a 1,000-pound bomb could collapse a ten-storey apartment block, and after that it took a week to get down to the ground floor and cellars where most people would have hidden when they first heard the scream of the jets. It was something they never seemed to learn: you only hid in basements or in corridors when *shells* were coming in. Shells hardly ever had the explosive force to collapse buildings, and anyway they came in at the sort of trajectory that just knocked holes in upper floors. But when the planes came (and you usually heard them – unless your building was the first target) you ran outside and got into sand-bagged bunkers if there were any, and if there weren't, you crouched close to walls so that if the explosion was close, the worst that could happen was that you got a wall fall all over you. You were better off lying flat on the open ground than in a cellar with eight or nine floors held up by crappy Beirut concrete above you.

Well if you're dead you're dead. What the fuck differ-ence does it make what way you go? If it's quick, you might just as well be buried under an office block as cut in half in the middle of Hamra. Well in theory yes, but after a while it all starts to get to you. You're sitting in the bar of the Commodore having the first cold beer of the day when you hear that jet-roar and the enormous thump, and you run through the lobby, into your car and tell the driver to head towards the plume of rising red dust; two minutes later there you are, screaming people running towards you, the crackle of A.K. fire as the militiamen try to clear the area; then you come round the corner, and there's the smoking pile of rubble and they're dragging the first bits and pieces out, piling them on stretchers, putting them into plastic bags. You go to about five or six of these little tributes to American ordnance and the Israeli air force, and it starts to dawn on you that probably people deserve a bit more than this. You think of yourself: you've got a family that wonders what you're doing, and friends who enjoy seeing you, and Bond Street auctioneers who depend on you, and guys who open oysters for you in Scott's in Mount Street and you've got all those editors in New York who expect you to shovel in a few columns every week. You don't think about dying much, but you do have certain feelings of mortality which get reinforced from time to time – like when guys with guns stick pistols in your ear while you're trussed up on your own floor, or when you follow up a bombing raid in Ouzai on a fish restaurant where you used to eat red mullet and there where the kitchen used to be, you see a single leg, neatly cut off at mid-thigh and still wearing a reddish brown shoe with a gold buckle on it and an unmarked fawn sock. If you're going to die, you realize you want your

friends or your editors to know about it, if only because they'll stop worrying now that they know you've got the business and there's no use crying about it.

What you don't want to happen to you is to end up like those people in west Beirut: you don't want to end up as a single leg, or a foot on top of a pile of hamburger, or a blackened scarecrow with its head in the wrong place. You don't want to be something that people have to wear gloves to pick up, and masks so they can get close enough to more or less pour you into a plastic bag. You don't want to be one of those bundles piled with the other anonymous bundles into the earth-mover's scoop and tipped into a great hole in the barren ground. You want people to know at least that you've ceased existing, so they can fix an image of you in their memories – something that's very hard to do when you're not sure whether a person is really dead or not. You like to think that your friends will hear about you and order another beer and say something like, 'Pity about poor old Tone being blown away like that. Silly fucker, he'd been going to wars for the past twelve years, he must have known the law of averages would get him some time. You can't get away with it for ever, even when you're a cautious bugger like he was. Trouble with Beirut was you couldn't be cautious, you didn't have to go to the front line to get yourself done in. Look at old Tone, right

Beirut, 1975

outside the office, not a plane in the sky, no shelling going on, and he gets blown to bits by a car-bomb.'

Just a scenario, of course, that last bit . . . yet I could easily have been blown to bits, just like that. Late in the war the Israelis and the Christians started using a lot of car-bombs. They're perfect terror weapons because you can pack a lot of explosive into a car, you can park it right where you want it to explode and because there is no warning at all, you blow dozens of people to pieces and rip the guts out of everyone's morale, because they never know when the mere act of stepping into the street is going to mean their own death. One favourite tactic was to use two cars and stagger the explosions. The first one would go off and kill a few people; a crowd of militiamen and civilians and ambulance men would gather, and then the second one would get them. If I'd been in the big black book for Beirut, I could easily have got it the day they decided to demolish the *An Nahar* newspaper building (where I worked) and the Information Ministry, which were opposite each other in Hamra. Normally, I would cross between the two at least once a day. The day I stayed alive was the day a guard at the Information Ministry saw a pretty girl park her car outside and then run for her life. He went out to the car: the thing was packed with plastic explosive with the clock running. The bombers were so confident that all that would be left would be a blood-smeared crater in the centre of a mountain of wrecked buildings that they hadn't even bothered to take the Hebrew-printed wrappers off the blocks of explosive. What's the Hebrew for 'A present from Arik and Menny'?

I may be kidding myself, but I like to think that if I didn't come back from somewhere, my friends would first worry and then come looking for me and probably find me, head or no head, because I'd be the only fat white corpse in a Saigon-made safari suit among all the brown corpses in their suits and jeans with Arabic labels. Someone might even write a piece about me ('you always get a nice notice in your own paper, and they always spell your name right – in the second edition', was almost the first piece of advice I got when I began work as a trainee on the Melbourne *Herald*). I would hope – no, let's not be modest, I would *expect* – that people would care if I died or not, that they would try to find out what had happened to me if I disappeared, and that my death would be noted by some and mourned by others – if not as a friend, then as a journalist.

If you were a Palestinian or a poor Lebanese refugee crowded into Beirut in the middle of 1982, you could expect none of these things. People driven from the south by the war often went first to the camps, especially if they were Palestinian but they were almost immediately driven out of the camps by the bombing, and in the end grabbed living space where they could. The lucky ones took over apartment blocks and office blocks, usually deserted by Lebanese owners who were able to quit Beirut if they chose and to pass out through the Christian checkpoints in the east of the perimeter to safety. The Palestinians were trapped as much by their accents as anything. They were totally uprooted; they had left everything behind them, they were total strangers in a strange city, usually huddling together with people they did not know. There was no one to miss them, no one to worry about why they did not come home at night and no way to check whether they were alive or not. If your father did not come home one night after a day spent fighting – or searching for food, for that matter – you couldn't call the police and report him missing. If he didn't come back, you could at least check with his militia friends if he was a fighter, but if he had just gone out for a coffee or to try and get some flour and didn't come back, you simply had to go to the area where you believed he had gone and start asking if there had been any attacks that day. And if there had, you then had to do the rounds of the hospitals and makeshift morgues, trying to find out whether he was wounded or at least had died cleanly enough for someone to store his body for a day, rather than just shovel it into the nearest crater and let the bulldozer cover it.

In those days, there simply wasn't anyone to care about the dead; they were in gross over-supply and they were shovelled under, the way French farmers bury tons of tomatoes and artichokes in years of glut because there are so many that nobody wants them. There were anonymous corpses buried under wreckage all over Beirut when the war ended, just as now there are thousands of people who will go to their graves wondering what happened to friends and relatives who said goodbye one day and never came back.

In one of the bloodiest bombings of the war the Israelis totally destroyed a building in the Rue Assi – the eight-storey apartment block near the Sanayeh Gardens that comes to mind again and again as I write. It was hit by a sortie of two planes and collapsed totally. This was the bombing which was so accurate that nothing else in the area was touched, and rumour had it that Arafat had been seen going into it less than an hour before the planes hit it. It would be no surprise to learn that he had been in the area, because both the nearby Sanayeh Gardens and buildings in the area, including this one, were filled with refugees; the disintegrated building was ironically, populated by Christian Arabs who had fled early in the civil war from the Christian Palestinian camp of Jisr al Basha, which was overrun and destroyed a few months before Tal Zaatar. The Rue Assi building was wrecked so utterly that hardly anybody got out of the wreckage alive and its pulverization led to rumours that the Israelis had some terrifying new 'vacuum bomb' that somehow imploded rather than exploded and therefore sucked in the walls of buildings, causing them to collapse. Nobody knows exactly how many people were killed there, but the Palestinians claimed around 260, and it is certain that more than 100 people died. The rescuers scrabbled desperately in the wreckage for days, looking for bodies and for still-living people. As with all the many collapsed buildings in west Beirut, it was a nearly impossible job because there were so few heavy earth-moving machines and so many buildings to dig out. To save many of the people who were alive under the wreckage of these buildings, the sites should have been dug out immediately with bulldozers, earth-movers and heavy cranes. As it was, you rarely saw more than one machine labouring away, while all but the heaviest work was done by main force: hundreds of people sometimes, manhandling great lumps of shattered concrete with their bare hands and listening all the time for the planes to come back.

Catherine grew obsessed by the destruction of the building in Rue Assi; it seemed to her (as it did to me) that the Israelis, on the off chance of hitting Yasser Arafat, had wantonly killed 100 civilians . . . or maybe 200 or 300. She was on the scene before the dust of the bombing had cleared; and she would go back day after day to take pictures and watch the volunteers desperately trying to move away the great slabs of concrete in their search for the living and the dead. 'The work would start about five-thirty each day – as soon as there was light enough to see. There was an earth-mover working, and a crowd of thirty or forty people gathered on the edge of the site. The earth-mover would grind in and scoop up a great load of earth and rubble and carry it out to the edge of the site, and dump its load on the ground. The crowd would rush forward to pick through the wreckage for the bodies of their relatives and friends. Most times, there would be nothing, but every third or fourth time there would be a body. They were hardly recognizable as human bodies, just blackened mashed-up bundles – and of course, none had any recognizable features. The people would have to search for things they could recognize: a medallion around a neck, a ring on a hand, maybe a dress or a jacket. The workers on the site had masks and gloves on to protect them from the smell and infection from the rotting flesh, but the people waiting would have to search through this mess with their bare hands.

'I photographed this drama every day, for a week or more. You would see people rush forward and suddenly someone would find something they recognized, a ring or an I.D. card or something like that; and women would start crying. After a while, I began to recognize faces in the crowd, and I became aware of a teenage boy, maybe about eighteen, in green military fatigues, who was always there and always with a much smaller boy who would hold his hand or sit very close to him. I couldn't be sure if they were brothers, or if the older boy was just looking after the younger one. I still don't know why they were there, but I suppose it was because one of them had a friend or some of his family in the ruins. After about four days, the elder one came to me and asked me, not angrily, but very calmly: "Why are you taking all these pictures, you are here every day taking

photographs?" And I thought for a minute and then I said: "I'm taking these pictures so that things like this won't be forgotten." '

As she said, she still remembers every word of his reply: 'Why shouldn't it be forgotten? Who cares? Nobody cares about us. They'll keep doing this to us, again and again and again. You're wasting your time here.'

You start to ask yourself questions when people say things like that to you. Were we all wasting our time in Beirut in 1982; do reporters actually ever do anything that moves world opinion enough to stop suffering of the magnitude that was inflicted on Beirut? We weren't wasting our time journalistically, of course: we were reporting the biggest story of the year; we got big play in our newspapers and magazines and on television around the world; we got bonuses and plaudits when we got back and, looking back on it, I am proud to have been in Beirut with a group of brave reporters who cared very deeply about what was being inflicted on the city and its people.

But did we change anything; could we look back and say that what we wrote saved a single life? . . . Six months later, it's hard to find much evidence that we did. We wrote that the Israelis were using cluster-bombs . . . we wrote that they were using white phosphorus . . . we wrote that their shelling and bombing was almost always indiscriminate . . . we wrote how hospitals seemed to have become major targets . . . we wrote about the way cluster-bombs were blanketing the city and how at least eighty per cent of those killed and wounded were civilian. We told the world that we believed that the Israelis were cutting off power and water and food, and that the first sufferers were going to be the children.

So what? No country protested by breaking off relations with Israel . . . no country declared that it would sell no more arms to Begin . . . certainly nobody had the guts to make a stupendous gesture like sending in an unarmed hospital ship to Beirut Harbour to take out civilian casualties. These would have been gestures – but they would have shown that somewhere out there, someone had absorbed the message we were all writing from Beirut. More than anyone, the Americans should have known, because most of the journalists working in Beirut were American, and most of the ordnance being dumped on us was American-made and brought to us via American planes and through American gun barrels. If Ronald Reagan watches television news, he must mentally edit out the nasty bits. I saw most of the film that was shot, and I can still cry over some of it, six months later. When he finally got mad, after 'Horrendous Thursday', 12 August when the Israeli air force bombed Beirut from morning to night, it was far too late. The shelling and bombing on that Thursday was an act of simple murderous vandalism and it finally irritated even Ronald Reagan into ringing up Begin.

'Mr Prime Minister,' he said, 'we have been very

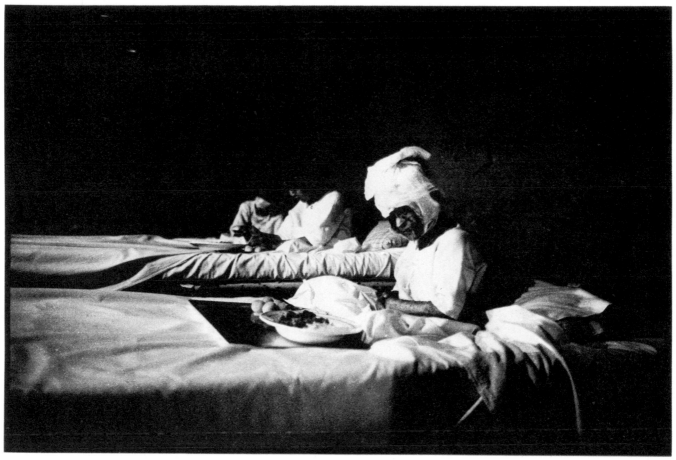

Beirut, 1976

patient, and this country has been very patient. But these bombings are getting to the point where they could seriously affect our long-term relationship,' and he ended by saying, 'I want it stopped, and I want it stopped now.' Begin then stopped – but not because of Reagan, because his troops had done their job. Reagan had been impotent to stop Begin before all the damage and death were inflicted.

Impotent like the rest of us, I guess. All our pleading and hard work didn't save anyone, it didn't shorten the war by a day; and even though we warned it might happen, we didn't prevent the massacres in the camps afterwards. We didn't do any worse than anyone else – after all, Philip Habib wasn't able to stop the war; like us, he ran frantically from place to place, getting nowhere; unlike us, he was credited with ending a war which in fact ran its natural course; it just happened to end when Habib was in the area, because its objectives had been achieved.

I'm glad the main reason for my working in journalism is that I have to make a living somehow. If I was in it purely to save the world, I would be damn-near suicidal

by now. I was in Biafra for a while and wrote about how people suffered there; I was in India and Bangladesh for the whole of 1971 and wrote yards of horror stories about the Pakistanis' campaign of murder against the Bengalis, but nobody took any notice of what hundreds of us hacks were saying; I was in Thailand, talking to the refugees driven out of Cambodia, and I finally got round to writing about the murder campaign there (most people wrote it better than I did but, between us, we let the world know). The world wrung its collective hands but did nothing, although it knew Cambodia was awash with blood from end to end, yet when the Vietnamese went in to clean out the murderers, they weren't praised but called 'invaders' – which was what a lot of people called the Indian army when it finally interrupted the Pakistani blood-bath in 1971. If you look at our record, we hacks are nothing but Cassandras: we tell the world what is happening, but nobody believes us or, if they do, they take no action. Maybe the boy who told Catherine she was wasting her time in the Rue Assi in 1982 was right . . . but I keep on trying to convince myself he is wrong.

'Tough Cats'

4

True Fedayeen

Driving from east Beirut to west Beirut in 1982 was like tiptoeing through ranks of sleeping crocodiles; you moved as silently as possible, so that you wouldn't disturb them – before you were able to throw yourself into a river full of piranhas. You drove through streets filled with Israeli and Phalangist soldiers, past jeeps loaded with communications equipment, past ranks of armoured personnel carriers, and finally past the big yellow-brown Merkava tanks with the machine-guns and massive 105-mm. gun, and on through a couple of hundred yards of no-man's-land, the muscles of your back twitching, before you reached the high piles of red earth topped with silk Palestinian flags that marked the beginning of the west Beirut defences. And behind the battlements? No tanks, no A.P.C.s, no communications centres: just a pack of teenage kids with A.K.-47s over their shoulders, an occasional jeep with a recoil-less rifle, and a few more kids lounging in the shade, R.P.G. rocket-launchers propped up against the wall beside them. The defenders of fortress Beirut, and when you looked them over you were most strongly reminded of that line of the Duke of Wellington's about the British army at Waterloo. All right, altogether now: 'They may not frighten the enemy but, by God, they frighten me.'

Well, it *was* a frightener. I'd prepared for Beirut before I left England by watching the television coverage of the war; what struck me more than anything, as I watched from my rocking chair with a beer in one hand and a pen in the other, was the sheer weight of firepower the Israelis had organized around Beirut. I would watch the 175- and 155-mm. artillery pieces up in the hills above Beirut pouring shells into the city, first the boom of the cannon and then, a second or two later, the red flash and puff of white smoke as the shell crashed into densely packed buildings in the south-western suburbs.

Then the film might cut to the tanks, and you'd hear the flat bang of the tank guns being fired and see those fifty-ton monsters shudder under the recoil. Another night, the film would be of air attacks: the tiny planes roaring across the screen, the bombs, just dots at that range, tumbling out of their bellies, then the huge fountain of white smoke and red dust below. From London, you wondered how the defenders of west Beirut had managed to hold out so long. When you actually got amongst them, you wondered why they had held out at all.

When it came down to it, west Beirut was defended successfully by a pack of kids under the direction of their fathers, uncles and elder brothers. For the first time in an Arab–Israeli war, the Arabs were outnumbered five to one by the Israelis in Beirut, and their equipment – well, their equipment reminded me of that old joke about the man who leaves his starving companions in the desert to look for food. He comes back and says 'I've got bad news and good news. The bad news is that all I could find to eat was camel shit. The good news is that there's tons of it.' So it was with the Palestinians and their Lebanese and Syrian allies in Beirut. To take on one of the best-equipped armies in the world, supported by an enormously powerful air force and an efficient little navy, the defenders of Beirut had only rifles, mortars, rocket-launchers, machine-guns and recoil-less rifles – but they had thousands of tons of them. They also had a few Russian tanks which were so old that back where they were made, they are usually cemented into war memorials celebrating the end of the Second World War, and some hand-cranked anti-aircraft guns with a range and manoeuvrability that would have made them deadly against Sopwith Camels. The artillery, such as there was of it, was almost entirely useless because of its lack of range and because the gunners trapped inside the city had no forward observers to tell them where the targets were and whether they were hitting them or not. They did in fact score the odd hit but, militarily, these were unimportant. What finally stopped the Israelis was lack of will on their part and a lot of kids on the other side who wcrc prepared to die, if that was what was needed to stop the tanks advancing.

What made their stand all the more remarkable was that when they finally drew back to west Beirut, the Palestinians were a well-beaten group of fighters. There is no question at all that they seriously misread Israeli intentions when the Israelis crossed the border on 6 June. It's not that they didn't expect an attack; Arafat had told me more than once that they knew the Israelis would turn on a repeat of the 1978 invasion. Where they got it wrong was in not realizing the Israelis were going to come across in such force, and they didn't think they were going to roll all the way to Beirut. They were waiting for the sort of short punitive campaign the Israelis had launched in 1978, and they were simply steamrollered by the massive wave that came at them.

I had covered the 1978 invasion, and the Palestinians had done pretty well – in the sense that they hadn't panicked, they'd kept in the field under fire for longer than the massed Arab armies in the Six Day War, they were still there when the Israelis stopped moving forward and they had fought gallant and almost suicidal actions to hold on to strongpoints like the famous Beaufort Castle, a Crusader fortress overlooking south Lebanon. A Palestinian friend who went there shortly after that battle said that the two sides had fought a pitched battle, and at the finish only the weight of the Palestinian dead and wounded piled against it had kept the main gate from being opened. The survivors were lying there, waiting for the last push, when the Israelis pulled out. Generally though, there had been no major battles; on the one or two occasions when I was down there and the Israeli tanks and troops started to move, the Palestinians would simply leave their positions and move slowly back out of range. The other feature of that particular struggle was that the Israelis didn't use too much heavy artillery and used the air force very sparingly. In retrospect, they obviously never planned a major invasion: they didn't try to take Tyre, for example. They were basically clearing out a piece of ground so that their Lebanese puppet, the former army major Saad Haddad, could set up his own little kingdom.

The trouble with the Palestinians is that when the fighting was over they thought they had won the Third World War, thrown back one of the world's most powerful armies and achieved a victory that the whole combined Arab armies, navies and air forces had never been able to do. So they were almost eager for the next round. Trouble was, next time the Israelis did all the things they hadn't done in 1978 and knocked hell out of them. First, they did their homework, they infiltrated

the area with agents, suborned local Palestinian leaders by bribery or threats, found out where the Palestinian strongpoints were, where the P.L.O. command posts were situated, where they had their supply dumps, where the P.L.O. commanders lived. Then they just swamped the area with men and armour and, if there were pockets of resistance like Beaufort, they just called in the air force and reduced it to rubble (one of the first chunks of television film I saw after the invasion started was of Israeli tourists being shown round the pulverized ruins of the Castle, and I suppose it says something for the Crusader architects that some of the arches and walls were still standing after all that). The whole episode was

found it hard to believe Yasser Arafat before the invasion when he said he could hold the south, it was much harder now to believe him when he said that Beirut was a different proposition and would not fall.

I'm not sure that I ever really believed that the Palestinians would hold the south against the Israeli hordes, but I thought that if they could hold Beirut for the first couple of weeks and regain their breath while the Israelis lost their momentum, they could probably hold the city. Once they got to the southern suburbs they were on home ground and were a lot more comfortable than when they had been stuck out in the open, down south. They also had the support of their families and

a total disaster for the Palestinians. They lost their empire in southern Lebanon, of course, but, more importantly, they lost thousands of men as prisoners, including some of their best commanders, thousands of tons of equipment and, worst of all, they were utterly defeated. The confident fighters who believed they had beaten off the Israelis in 1978 were simply rolled over by a mass of men and armour that took just eight days to get from the frontier of Israel to the outskirts of Beirut. The Palestinian remnants fleeing ahead of them arrived back in west Beirut with the news that they had been totally unable even to slow down the Israeli advance. If you had

were close to their friends. When they were down in the orange groves they had very serious communications problems: their electronics weren't so good, so that often they were completely out of touch, and when they did manage to get through they were probably being intercepted half the time and their movements were piped straight down to Tel Aviv. In Beirut, they were all within a mile or two of one another; instead of shouting down rickety two-way radios, they could drive round to their forward posts in a couple of minutes to deliver orders and messages personally. It was one of the miracles of the war that the phone system in Beirut never broke down entirely, so commanders could keep contact by phone if necessary. We had friends who were fighters and they could leave front-line positions after telling their friends they were going up to the Commodore for dinner. We'd be sitting around with Baha and Ali and Mustafa around eleven at night, when the paging system would burst into life; it would be someone like Kalil down near Ouzai asking the lads to come back and bring their guns with them because they were getting incoming mortar rounds. The morale of men who know their friends and families are literally just round the corner is bound to be higher than that of miserable little bands huddled among the olive trees south of Sidon, waiting

first couple of weeks, before the lines stabilized, were very uncertain ones. There they were, outnumbered five to one, with their rotten little guns, in a rough rectangle with the sea on the north and west sides, the Israelis in the south, and the Israelis and the Christians in the east. Their job was made simpler by the fact that they didn't have to worry about trying to break out to freedom because, if they somehow managed to push through the perimeter, they would only expose themselves to the massed Israeli guns and planes as they tried to make it to the mountains. All they had to do was hold the line, and they did. Early on, they thought that they wouldn't have to do the job on their own; they sincerely believed the

for some bloody great Phantom to fly over and unload six tons of assorted ordnance on their heads.

There was also the incentive of knowing that they had to fight, because there was nowhere else to go. When the Palestinians took the final decision to make their last stand in Beirut rather than split up and try to leak out to Syria, they knew they would have no choice but to fight to the end. Guerrilla armies shouldn't make last stands; but the Palestinians had close to 200,000 Palestinian civilians and 250,000 Lebanese to protect, and they couldn't just save their own skins and leave their friends and families and supporters behind. Nevertheless, the

Arab brothers wouldn't sit around and let the Israelis slowly grind them into dog-food. These hopes disappeared pretty soon; the Arabs told them very quickly that there was going to be no camel corps galloping over the hill to rescue Fort Arafat. 'Tough shit,' came the message clearly from the Mediterranean to the Gulf.

The men doing the fighting never wasted their breath abusing Begin or Sharon; but you couldn't measure the bitterness they felt towards the Arabs and the Russians, because they believed that these 'allies' had completely sold them down the river. 'Pity they hadn't been killed,' said the Marxist Palestinian leader, Nayef Hawatmeh, when he heard that two Russian diplomats had been injured by an Israeli shell – and the Russian Ambassador had a temper tantrum and wouldn't see Hawatmeh for almost a month, although the Russians had until then spent hours in the Commodore telling us what a sound little fellow Hawatmeḥ was. The Pals didn't expect Brezhnev to come galloping over the hills in person at the head of a squadron of Cossacks, but they hoped the Russians might show more anxiety about what was going on by doing something fairly aggressive, like mooring some ships off Beirut, on the grounds that they were concerned for the lives of Soviet citizens attached to the Embassy, or moving mobile troops like paras to, say, Damascus for the same sort of reason. In the end the Russians sat on their hands, and the Arab brothers did the same.

In the second month of the fighting I was doing a story about 'the Palestinians' and talking to the usual suspects about their lives and hopes; one day I was talking with Mwein Bsiso, a well-known Palestinian poet who had been jailed – not by the Israelis, but by the Egyptians, of all people – for his subversive activities on behalf of the Palestinians in Gaza. He was talking about the way the Palestinians had been betrayed once again, something that came as no surprise to him at all. He is a tall, handsome, gaunt man with long flowing grey hair; he chain-smokes, sucking on cigarettes as if they were his only source of oxygen.

He was talking about the irony of it all: 'What a black comedy this all is. I've just heard that the wives of Arab ambassadors have gone on hunger strike in Washington in protest about what is happening here – but I have yet to hear that a single Arab oil-well has gone on strike. When you review what is happening here, the bitterest irony of all is that the greatest demonstrations against this monstrous war are taking place not in Tripoli or Jeddah or Amman; they're taking place in Israel. They got one crowd of 100,000 people to demonstrate against the war in Tel Aviv – you tell me which city in the Arab world has protested on a scale like that.'

So, in the end the Palestinians and their Lebanese allies did it on their own; by 'did it', I mean they didn't lose the war and they got their forces out to fight another day, which is what guerrilla armies are supposed to do. Part of the wonder is that they managed to do that against one of the most powerful armies in the world; next, that they did it with what was basically a bunch of teenage kids using the sort of weapons that were in theory totally useless against what they were facing – which was heavy tanks, the best air force America could give them, and artillery with such a range that the gunners could eat sandwiches out in the open between rounds because they knew the defenders of Beirut could never reach them with the rubbish they had to use themselves.

In the end, the reason the Pals held out is that both sides lived up to the assessments made by every

journalist infesting the Commodore bar. This assessment was that the Pals would indeed fight to the last man if necessary because they had nowhere else to go; their alternative to fighting was being killed by the Phalangists or led away to captivity and humiliation by the Israelis. We also concurred that the Israelis would

'The Last Barricade', Ouzai

not go the last mile, because they weren't prepared to die for it. Just for once, the bar-flies got it right, and most of us wrote at some point a story which read something like this: 'The question is whether the Israelis are prepared to take the casualties they know they will suffer if they move into the crowded streets of west Beirut. The

Palestinians will stand and fight, and when they do the Israelis will have to leave their cumbersome tanks which become sitting ducks for anti-tank rockets when they are trapped in narrow streets, and go after the enemy on foot. When this happens the two sides will be so close together the Israelis will not be able to use the air and artillery support which normally flattens everything between them and their targets. On foot the Israelis will be operating in streets they do not know, against an enemy who has lived in these crowded buildings and alleys all his life. The Israelis are not cowards but coming from a country with a very small population, they are extremely sensitive about losing men and have always preferred to fight with machines. For the first time in its military history Israel will be fighting inside a major city; and it is an axiom of war that both sides in house-to-house fighting take heavy casualties . . .' and so on and so on, all good stuff, if prosaic as hell and as it turned out, completely true.

When I went back after the war, Catherine took me to meet her friend Farouk, a Palestinian fighter who had been operating with a small team of Palestinians and Lebanese on the airport perimeter, one of the hottest parts of the whole line. We eventually found him at his home in Bourj Barajneh after half the neighbourhood had given us wrong directions about where to find him. (We'd been misdirected because he had been picked up by the police several times since the end of the war; when we saw him, he had just been released again from a jail in east Beirut where as he said, he had spent most of his time being beaten up by the guards who kept telling him in a kindly sort of way that they'd stop playing football with his head as soon as he said Palestine was a whore.) Farouk was a short, very powerfully built young man, with big shoulders and short heavy thighs like a rugby scrum half. He was the sort of kid the British police normally call 'a right little tearaway'; he had a cocky manner and had his own little gang around him even now that the war was over, and seemed to be driving a different car every time I saw him. One day it would be a battered Mercedes, the next a B.M.W. with the mudguards ripped off. He was also very bright, spoke beautiful English and wrote poetry in English in the quiet times in his bunker . . . the sort of man who in a normal city might become a successful politician or even a successful gang-leader.

He drove us back to the Commodore to talk because we were attracting far too much attention in that little back street in Bourj Barajneh. During the war it had been a stronghold of the Palestinian and Lebanese leftists, but now there were police all over the place and strangers flying Lebanese flags on their cars whom nobody trusted. The locals had sensibly taken on protective colouring and this once fiercely anti-Phalangist enclave was a mass of red and white Lebanese flags hanging from cables stretched across the street; shops I knew were owned by Palestinians had their windows plastered with the picture of the new president, Amin Gemayel, and his assassinated brother Bashir. Everyone had been made very nervous by repeated police raids and Farouk said he had no doubt that half a dozen people had carefully noted the sudden presence of two Europeans loaded with cameras and notebooks.

Farouk must have been about twenty-one when I met him, and by that time he had been a military man for well over half his life. He was proud of the fact that he was in the first group of young Palestinians sent abroad for military training; when he was eight he had become a very junior volunteer, a '*shibel*', or lion-cub as they were called, and had been sent to Baghdad for weapons training along with his younger brother who was only six. They were taught self-defence and how to use machine-guns; they already were used to Kalashnikovs, and were there for almost six months. At ten, Farouk had graduated to training in firing heavy artillery although, as he says, he was too small to be able to lift a single shell. He looked back to those years like some ancient pensioner remembering Waterloo and said, 'In those days we were true *fedayeen*, we really wanted to die for Palestine, it meant something to us then. I volunteered to go even when I was as young as that, I wasn't pushed by anyone. My mother tried hard to stop me because she said I was too young to leave home, and although my father wanted me to go and was proud when we left he didn't force us in any way.'

He started talking about the siege, and the first thing he said was something I had heard from nearly all the fighters I had spoken to throughout the war: 'Do you know, in all the fighting I never saw an Israeli soldier. I saw their tanks and A.P.C.s and planes, but never a man. They would never come out in the open to get us – they were frightened to leave their machines. It made things much easier for us because if you knew you were in an area where the tanks couldn't come because of the rough ground, you knew you would have an easy time. Do you know, I often got closer than a hundred metres to tanks and I never saw a soldier, not even one head looking out of a tank.'

I asked him if he had felt frightened in the 1982 siege when he saw the tanks coming; he said he hadn't and then seeing that I thought he was talking tough, he went on to explain: 'I was in the P.F.L.P. in 1978 when the Israelis invaded the south, and I told my father I wanted to go and fight. He said he wouldn't let me because all my friends had been killed; but I went anyway and I ended up in a place called Saksikieh in front of Bourj Ismaili. We were in groups of three, I was carrying the R.P.G.-7 launcher, there was another guy carrying the rockets, and the third one had grenades and his A.K.-47. We were on flat open ground one night, and we had just come out of the olive groves; ahead of us was a rise and there were two or three Israeli tanks moving along it. I remember it was pouring with rain and the mud stuck to our boots as we ran – the only cover was a few little stone huts, and as we ran our boots got heavier and heavier – each one felt as if it weighed about ten kilos. We were in the storeroom of this little stone house and I think we would have let the tanks go by but there was this big whoosh and a bang and a tank shell hit the hut and the man with the rifle was killed. They knew we were there,

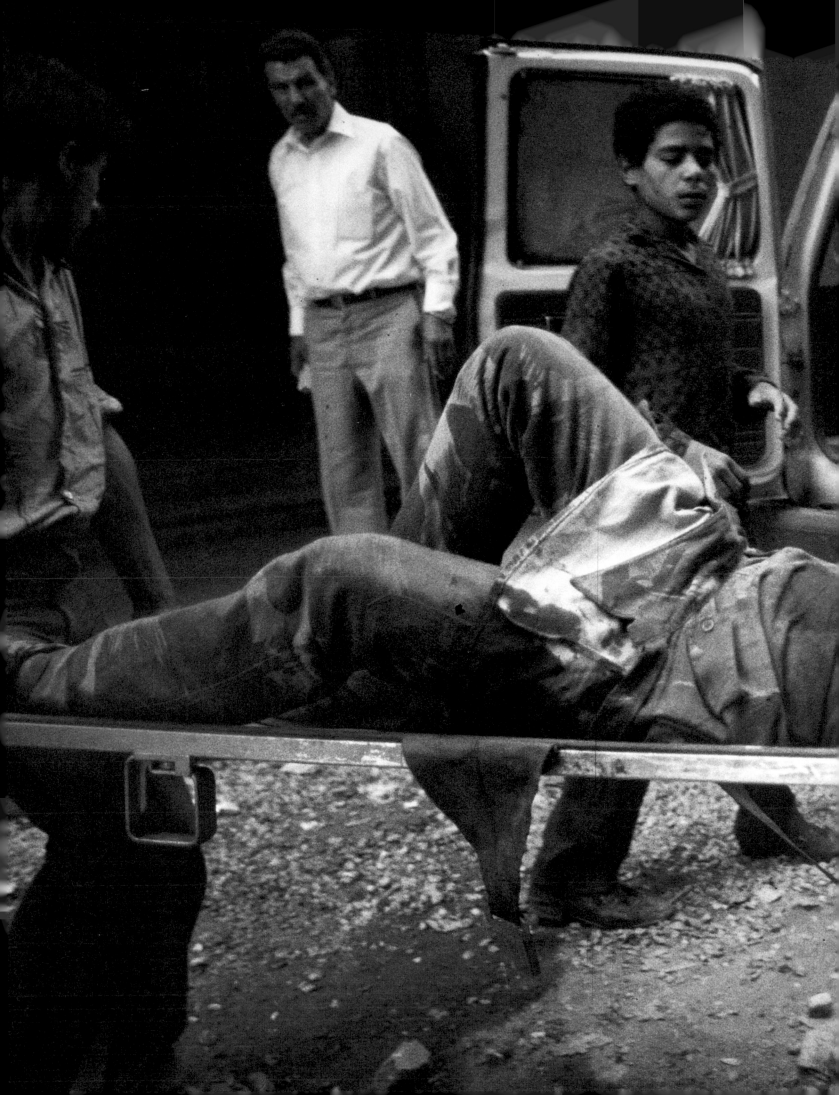

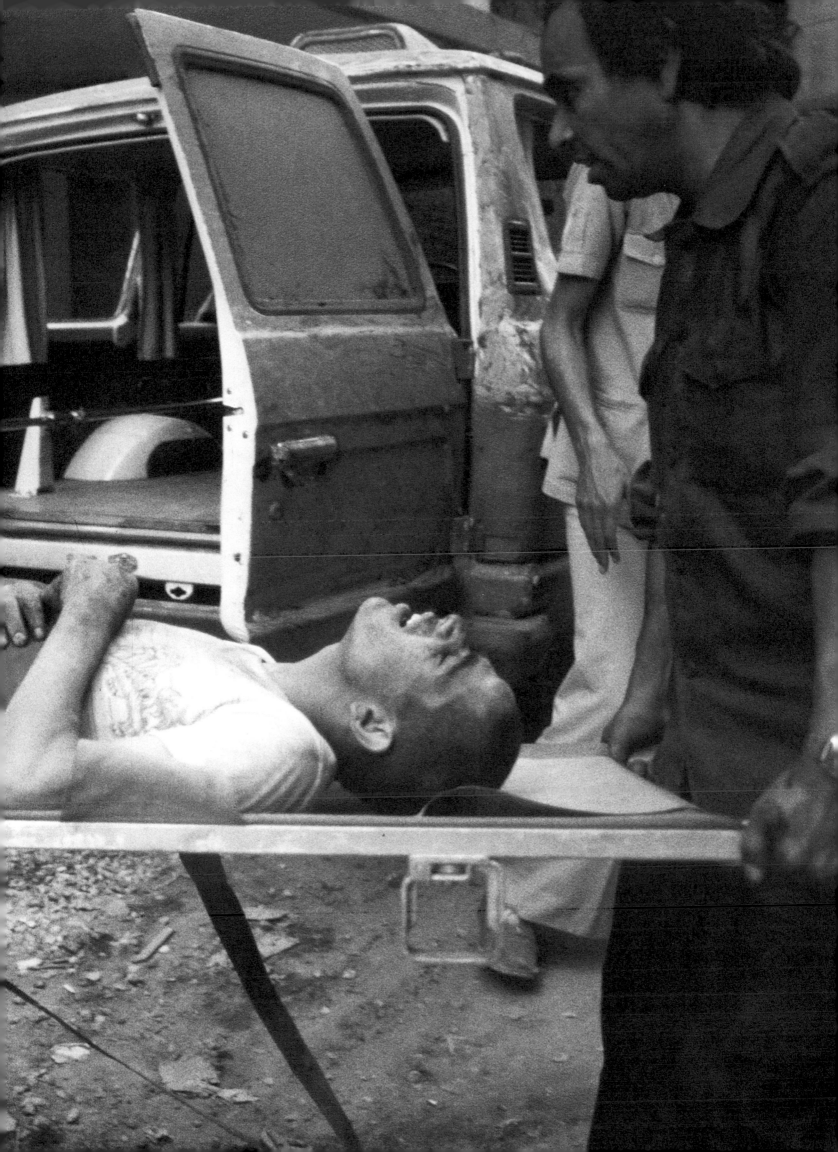

so we had to get out of the place.

'We were so close that in the little bit of moonlight I could see the tank commander on the lead tank looking around with his infra-red binoculars. I kept trying to remember all the rules about attacking tanks. You were told never to get behind one to fire because you would be picked up by the machine-gun on the one following him, and you were told to try not to get in front of one because there was thick armour on the front and the machine-gun and main gun were usually trained straight ahead, so that if you missed with your first shot they'd get you with one or the other. We were taught we should always try to get round and fire from side-on, because the side gave you the biggest target. The best side was the left side because that was where they stored their ammunition and if you got a good hit there, the whole tank would blow up at once.

'So we ran out, crouching down to escape attention, and the tank suddenly turned towards us; I don't know if they had seen us or not. I was half kneeling and I could see the tank's gun swinging around and I was so terrified I couldn't stand up. I don't think he had seen us because the gun swung past us and I forced myself to stand up and fire. I hit somewhere in the back of the turret I think, and maybe I hit some ammunition. Anyway there was an explosion and the thing started to burn and we turned and ran. I dropped the rocket-launcher in the mud and we ran madly for the olive trees because we knew if we could make it to the cover we would be safe. We managed to scramble back and our leader said that if I could hit a tank every time I fired he wouldn't mind how many rocket-launchers I lost. When I think back, I can't imagine how I hit it because the front of a tank is a small target, especially in the rain, and I was shaking so much with fear that the whole launcher was bobbing up and down. So the reason I wasn't frightened this year was that I had seen the Israeli tanks before and I knew what to do.'

In fact by the time the Israelis got to Beirut the guerrillas who had fallen back had all had some sort of experience of fighting. The ones from the south had just fought against the Israelis and the ones who had stayed to defend Beirut against either Phalangist pushes or Israeli surprise attacks from air or sea had fought the Israelis in 1978 or had had three years testing themselves against the Christian militiamen in the civil war. This experience hadn't turned them into the Afrika Korps, but it did mean that the defenders were the sort of men who didn't run away when they heard a mortar fired, because they'd all heard the sound before. They knew how to use the limited weapons they had, they knew they had huge stockpiles of guns and ammunition, and finally they knew they weren't going anywhere else. All they were able to do was prepare their positions, get comfortable in them and wait to see what the Israelis would do.

Until they hit Beirut, the Palestinians had been going backwards since day one. They didn't hold anywhere for longer than hours, although once again Beaufort Castle saw some vicious fighting which only ended when the Castle and its defenders were bombed almost to dust. There were brief heroic little fire-fights on both sides, and the kids with the R.P.G.s would hold fortified houses and bunkers for a few hours before the Israelis simply brought up air support or big guns and pulped them, but overall the guerrillas who held the Israelis to a draw at the Litani in 1978 were simply overwhelmed in 1982. After a week in 1978, the Israelis called it a day after they racked up a northward advance of under twenty miles. After a week in 1982 they had taken and half wrecked Tyre and Sidon and were panting outside the gates of Beirut, with Arafat and the rest of the high command trapped inside and their more panicky lieutenants thinking of final solutions ranging from mass suicide to getting into the Soviet Embassy and trying to force the Russians to send in their troops to defend them, and get them out under diplomatic truce.

I was not in Beirut when the Israelis surrounded the place, so I can only build a theory on what people told me later. But if I had to explain why the Israelis behaved as they did, I would say the pattern of their war would indicate they made a basic miscalculation about the fighting ability of the guerrillas in the city and also about the will of the Lebanese who decided they were not going to be bombed out of west Beirut. This is not meant to be a military history, but there are known facts about the siege, and I was there when it was at its worst. So here is the Clifton scenario of those momentous events in June, July and August.

The Israelis invaded on 6 June and probably to their own surprise, found themselves on the outskirts of Beirut by 14 June. There they stopped, dug in around the high points and near the major exits and entrances to the city, brought up their big guns and started to blow the bejesus out of the place. My own belief is that this happened because they had the Palestinians on the run and they calculated that the guerrillas' morale was so badly broken by their treatment in the south that all that was needed was a few days' bombing to produce a surrender. If Beirut had been the sole object of the war, they could have taken it then if they'd been prepared to make a sea- or helicopter-borne landing in the heart of the city; but I think that they didn't do that because they knew they would risk taking heavy casualties and they didn't think it worth losing men, especially in the beginning when all they had to do was wait a few days for the Pals to come marching out with their hands up. All their previous wars have shown the Israelis are not besiegers; they like to wrap things up as quickly as possible, but they like losing men even less than hanging about and in this case they were under no pressure to stop the killing because the rest of the world was sitting this one out.

After a couple of weeks of siege, it slowly began to

Street fighting, Beirut 1976. Training for 1982

dawn on Sharon and the generals that Yasser had mislaid his white flag and that he was quite prepared to sit in Beirut and wait for someone to come and get him. The Israelis had relaxed the initial pressure on the defenders; they weren't trying to get into Beirut and that gave the Palestinians and their Lebanese friends time to fortify their positions and hunker down under the shelling.

By the end of July it must have been clear even to the Israeli High Command that the Palestinians were not going to cave in; this is when they finally decided they would have to go in and winkle the defenders out. There

resoundingly – 'Horrendous Thursday'.

I think the first two were the really serious pushes, the third was just sheer blind rage and a final attempt to terrify people into giving up. But on Sunday and Wednesday the tanks and A.P.C.s came grunting and farting into action, trying to push in through the weakest parts of the perimeter, across the flat land in the south where the cleared area of the airport and the golf course ran into the Palestinian camps, through the road crossing-point at the museum and finally through the battered ruins of the port area. These were classic ground attacks. First, there was a huge artillery barrage that began in darkness and went on until close to dawn when the tanks and A.P.C.s started to move; then the air attack followed for most of the day. On 'Horrendous Thursday' they just started with air attacks at daybreak and accompanied by land and naval artillery, this went on all day. That was the day when they hit everything and damn near everybody, just lashing out blindly in all directions, blanketing the whole city with bombs and shells.

I worked very hard on Wednesday, 4 August. I had been around on the previous Sunday when the Israelis made their first charge, but I didn't go to watch the fun because it was past my deadline. I am very superstitious about going to dangerous places when I don't need to because two of my good friends, a stringer of ours called Alex Shimkin and a television cameraman called Terry Khoo, were both killed in Vietnam in actions they didn't need to be near. Alex had gone out on a Sunday to cover a small fire-fight because he was an obsessive student of war; his body has never been recovered. Terry had been posted to West Germany and had gone out simply to take a last look at the countryside where he had made his reputation; he got hit. I decided then that I would take risks if I had a chance of getting the story in the paper; otherwise I'd leave that sort of fun to the dailies. So while I knew there was a big push on the Sunday, I didn't go right up to the perimeter. Rather, I hung around the hotel and watched what was happening from the roof with binoculars. Even then it was a front row in the stalls and we were close enough to feel the hotel shudder as the 1,000-lb. bombs hit half a mile away down on the beachfront.

On Wednesday I actually got up and went down to the Museum Crossing. I suppose the most striking thing about what was happening is that I didn't really feel too threatened. The Israelis were trying to move tanks along the main road and through the racecourse grounds alongside it, but were not getting anywhere because of the R.P.G.-7 fire they were encountering. You felt more or less safe because the area being held by the Palestinians on the other side of the road from the race-track was packed solid with apartment blocks, so you could get to within a couple of hundred yards of the first tank and still have half a dozen concrete walls shielding you. I remember being surprised at how high the

were three very big Israeli actions: the first was on 1 August, which the Lebanese immediately christened 'Black Sunday'; the second was on 4 August, which was called 'Bloody Wednesday'; and the third and final shove was on 12 August – by then they were running out of striking titles, and this one was called – not very incoming fire was – as you walked through the streets you were showered with glass and concrete splinters from third and fourth floors – this would have been supporting artillery fire from the Israeli gunners behind the tanks. At the end of each road on our side were huge barricades of piled earth, some with old cars and trucks folded into them; these ten-foot-high walls of red dirt absorbed most machine-gun and sniper fire. The two sides were too close for the Israelis to call in air support, so that if you kept your head down you could sneak forward and reach a point where the tanks were pretty much just over the next pile of earth. But even as close as four hundred yards away you would find local residents, the odd middle-aged man in his pyjamas and teenage kids with portable radios, crouched up against the earth barriers with the guerrillas, occasionally peering over the top to see what the tanks were doing.

In fact the tanks weren't doing much. They came in, their turrets moving suspiciously from side to side like rhinos sniffing the wind, and about as cumbersome. The Palestinians would hammer away with heavy machine-guns and try to smash a link in a track, and then every now and again a kid with an R.P.G.-7 launcher would rush out, fire a round and duck back. Most of the rounds bounced off or missed completely and I never saw a tank explode, but they did get some hits; the advance down that axis after a day of very dedicated pushing and shoving never exceeded about 150 yards – a totally unimportant distance, given the terrain in that area. They also got stalled in the port for the same reason – the tanks couldn't manoeuvre in the narrow streets and when one stopped the whole advance stopped. The only breakthrough was in the open ground near the airport which was softened up first by air and artillery and had to be given up by the Palestinians because they just didn't have any cover. The real test, which never came, would have been if the Israelis had pushed past the outskirts of the camps and the new residential areas on the south coast a mile in from the airport, where the Palestinians could use the buildings as shields and the roads as tank traps. 'Bloody Wednesday' turned out to be as bloody for the Israelis as for the Palestinians – the Israelis admitted losing nineteen killed and about 160 wounded. They really tried that day; this was no tightening-the-noose operation – they sent the tanks and the A.P.C.s into very hot areas and they kept going all day, losing armour all through the daylight hours and, I suspect a lot of the casualties were men caught in the A.P.C.s stalled behind the knocked-out tanks.

As you watched a battle like that develop, it became clear that the Israelis had left their run much too late. The kids in the bunkers on our side had just had a month of shelling and by now they weren't going to get rattled by another attack. I say 'kids' meaning fighters under about twenty-three – and a lot of them were much younger than that. Most of us operated by getting to know one group very well and then using them as our

source of information about what was going on at the front. Catherine and I were especially friendly with a group on the southern perimeter commanded by a mid-ranking officer (probably around the rank of major in a regular army) called Mustafa who was in loose command of a group of Palestinian and Lebanese fighters in their

'I volunteered when I was as young as that' — Farouk

late teens and early twenties. Mustafa was about thirty-four and he had been fighting or politicking with Fateh, the main group in the P.L.O., since he was fifteen. He was a neat, small, muscular and very softly spoken man who was part fighting soldier and part political cadre, something between a father-figure and commander to the fighters with him; his grave manner certainly made him appear much older than he was, and the kids with him paid him the sort of respect that young Arabs are taught to show their fathers and men much older than Mustafa. He spoke very good English and we would sit in his position, eating water melon, arguing politics and trying to assess where the war would end. He would lead the conversations, but the fighters would drift in and out; every now and again one would pick up the thread of an argument, add his own thoughts and then move out, or sit and listen. There was no sense of officer and men, although when Mustafa gave orders they were obeyed immediately. But if someone disagreed with what was being said he didn't say 'Excuse me, sir' before adding his bit.

Mustafa's command post was on the ground floor of a half-completed fourteen-storey office block at the end of Corniche Mazra'a, the wide main road that sweeps along the southern side of west Beirut, from the sea all the way down to the museum – it was in fact the road the Israelis would have moved down if they had managed to break through at the Museum Crossing. The building was at the seaward end of the road, not at the front line but in an area where virtually every building had been hit repeatedly by shelling and bombing. The concrete skeleton of the building had been completed, and Mustafa and his men had sandbagged the ground and first floors, filling the area where the front windows of a ground-floor shop would be one day, and building up a parapet on the first floor to about waist high. This parapet had pots full of flowers balanced on it, and the kids would take great care to make the place look neat and clean – Catherine remembers going there one day during a barrage that shook the ground so much it threatened to throw her car off the road, and seeing Ali, one of the young Lebanese in the group, industriously sweeping the courtyard as concrete fragments from hits higher up the building showered down on him.

Mustafa's family had wanted him to be a doctor when he was a boy in Amman; his father was a clerk in a business there and like a lot of Palestinian parents – or Jewish for that matter – he wanted his son to have a respectable profession. Mustafa decided very young that doctoring was not going to get Palestine back and that if it came back at all it would come back because the Palestinians fought for it. 'We've got thousands of doctors,' he used to say, 'it's not doctors who are going to win back our country, it's fighters. That's one of the things I decided very early, and the other thing that I'm certain about is that international goodwill won't get us a state either. I could show you enough documents to

block that doorway, demanding we have a state. The United Nations has asked it, the Organization for African Unity has asked it, the Non-Aligned Movement has demanded it . . .' He'd make a dismissive gesture with one hand. 'All those pieces of paper – and not a square metre of land. If we're going to have a Palestine, we're going to get it in battle.'

He was one of those men who had studied every possible aspect of the history of the Palestinian question, so he knew whole areas of British history that I knew nothing about – I notice for instance that I have all sorts of notes about what Campbell-Bannerman said about a buffer state in the Middle East in 1911. He would start talking about the history of the Balfour Declaration and ask me what role I though British Zionists had played in getting the document signed and then I think, be slightly surprised when I said we hardly ever mentioned Balfour when I was at school and certainly never in the context of a Jewish state. These talks would go on for hours, in the command post, around the pool at the Commodore, Mustafa in his dark-green short-sleeved battle-dress, usually with a couple of the younger fighters listening intently and trying to eat slices of roast beef with forks and understand my Australian accent at the same time. Mustafa had been in Vietnam in 1980 for training with the North Vietnamese and I remember him saying once, after we'd had a few beers and talked half the night, 'I sometimes think we Palestinians have been much too soft. We spend too much time arguing and laughing and enjoying ourselves. The Vietnamese were so cold and hard – I never really got to be friendly with any of them, although I was an honoured guest – but they knew exactly what they had to do in the war against the Americans, and they fought and made terrible sacrifices, and they won. We worry about our children's education and about Arab unity and about our girl-friends – I sometimes wonder whether we shouldn't just forget everything and think about nothing but fighting until we get our state back. I wonder if one day history won't look at us and decide that we went in the wrong direction.'

At some point in these talks with people like Mustafa or Ali or Farouk, or with the political people like Abu Iyad or Mahmoud Labady, the question would always arise as to whether the Palestinians had had a victory over the Israelis in Beirut. After all they had stopped the Israelis dead, they had sat under that firestorm for two months and had not been moved and finally they would get out and go to the Arab countries where they could regroup and fight again. After two months, they were all realists. Mustafa thought about the question and then said, 'O.K., we had a negative victory. By that I mean the Israelis didn't get what they wanted, which was to get into Beirut and capture or kill us. But you can't call what we achieved here a victory – we didn't conquer the enemy – and that's what victory means.' Abu Iyad was asked the same question when he was doing the rounds

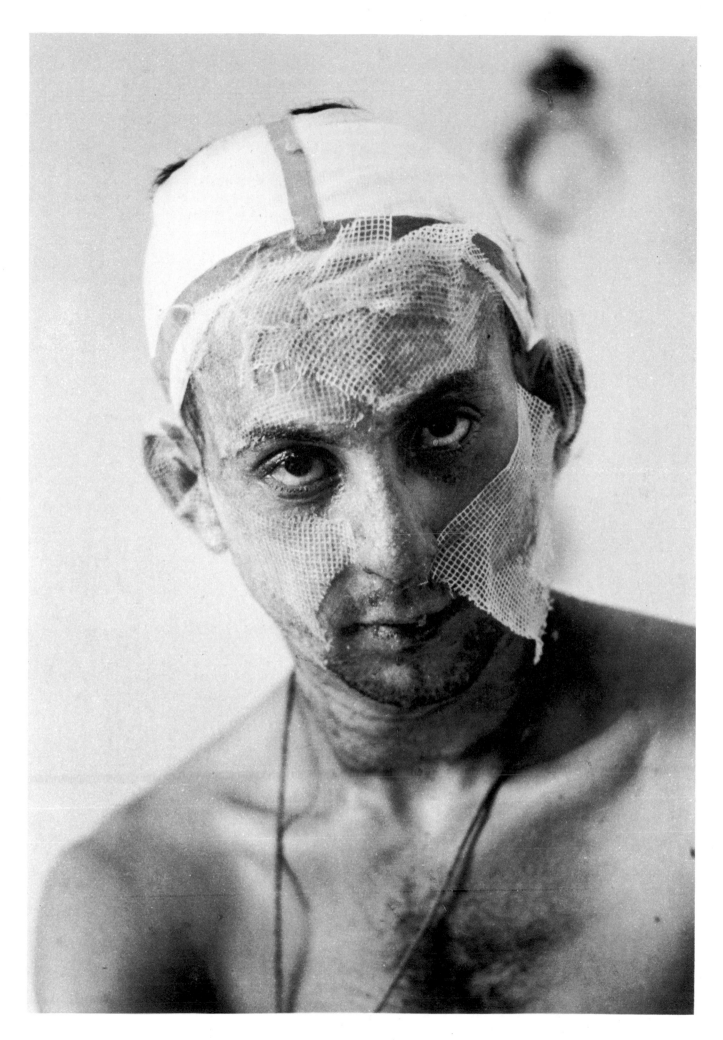

'I never saw an Israeli soldier' — Farouk

of Fakhani, the district near Corniche Mazra'a where the Palestinians had their offices and which was very heavily shelled and bombed. The reporters would sit around outside Labady's now doorless and windowless office waiting for the Palestinian leaders to appear – after six weeks of near misses they had become very security conscious and would never give notice of when, or even if, they were due to appear. But they would come: Arafat, Habash, Abu Jihad, Abu Iyad. Abu Iyad turned up in a maroon Mitsubishi one afternoon and drank a coffee among the ruins. He was asked about victory and turned the question into another: 'Did we fail when we stopped one of the best-equipped armies in the world getting into Beirut? They tried again and again and they couldn't move on the ground. Is this a defeat? We go with our weapons to continue the struggle else-where. It would be totally unfair to say this has been a defeat.' For someone like Mahmoud, who had spent the last ten years explaining to plane-loads of foreign journalists who Yasser Arafat was and where Palestine was situated in relation to the Mediterranean, what happened in Beirut '. . . is neither a victory nor a defeat. It's just another step along the road for us. We've been hunted out of Palestine, then out of Jordan, now out of Lebanon. We're getting our fighters out of here intact and we will just continue the fight somewhere else. The Israelis try to hunt us down and eliminate us while at the same time asking for world support for what they're doing, because they suffered in Europe in the 1940s. They're trying to do to us what the Nazis did to them, and they actually ask the world to feel sorry for them. We can't defeat Israel in battle, we can't even endanger them militarily, but this time we are endangering them morally. For the first time the world is seeing who the aggressors are, who the killers are, and we have its sympathy. Sympathy for us won't stop the Israelis trying to destroy us, but it should make a lot of people question why they always stood by Israel in the past, no matter what it did.'

I think that Mustafa's definition of victory is a reason-able one, that 'you conquer the enemy'. Israel didn't conquer the Palestinians in Beirut; they left with their leadership intact and went off to friendly countries (that's a fairly relative 'friendly', after what happened in Beirut, but it's close enough). Israel could only claim a victory in the sense that a man who pushes a stick into a hornets' nest to make them fly away to another tree could claim that he had solved his hornet problem. There are now something like 13,000 Palestinian guer-rillas brooding in camps all over the Middle East, from Syria to Shandi in Sudan, from Baghdad to Amman. They aren't frightened of the Israelis, they're bitter about leaving the only country many of them knew; some of them are lusting for good old biblical vengeance after what the Israelis allowed the Phalangists to do in Sabra and Chatila after they left. As much as anything, they're bored out of their minds because their new Arab

hosts are so frightened of them, they've sealed them into camps a long way from town and only let them out for the occasional weekend. These are all city kids who grew up in sophisticated centres like Beirut where they were used to going to the movies, drinking, getting laid and carrying guns. In Baghdad, when I was there in November, they were just starting a regime of heavy training in guerrilla warfare to keep them so tired they wouldn't go wild during their weekends off, and while I was there a story leaked out about how a group of kids in Shandi (which is approximately twenty-seven miles from nowhere) had stolen the local judge's car and wrecked it while trying to rob the local bank which they found was totally empty. Oh, and we were told, they also had to put armed guards on the local girls' school because the Palestinians used to hang round the place, waiting for some action. The last time I heard from Mustafa he was in Eastern Europe, or that's where the postcard was from. Another of his men, Samir, was in Paris; Farouk was lying low in Beirut, and I hope that kids like Baha and Ali and Khailal 'the Knight', who were also in Mustafa's group, are still alive either in Beirut or outside, although I have not heard anything of them in the two visits I have made to Beirut since the war ended. I want them to be alive because they became friends and looked after me and because I admire them as I admire nearly all fighting soldiers. It so happens that I support the Palestinians' fight for a homeland, but even if I had no feelings about it I would have been glad to count Mustafa, Baha, Farouk and the others as friends. You get the official claptrap and the ideology from the colonels and the politicians, but it is even more meaning-less when heard in someone's nice big office. When you hear the same thing from a man who you know is likely to be blown away in the next hour, it all takes on a new meaning. For that reason you had to respect the Lebanese volunteers in west Beirut more than anyone because they were fighting for a cause greater than simple survival. At the very lowest common denomi-nator, the Palestinians were fighting for their lives and their freedom, because if the Israelis had broken in they would have captured the guerrillas or killed them, either by themselves or using the Phalangists. The Lebanese on the other hand, could just have chosen not to fight and either got out through the checkpoints or sat in their houses waiting for the surrender. Instead, they fought alongside the Palestinians, drove ambulances and manned hospitals for motives which ranged from pure Lebanese nationalism – 'The Israelis aren't going to take my country' – to complex ideas of pan-Arabism and the need for all Arabs to unite against a common enemy. I think especially of Samir, a French-speaking Christian with Mustafa's group who would have been welcomed in east Beirut if he had got out at the beginning yet who chose to stay, knowing that if worse came to worst the hostility towards him would be twice as great as towards a Muslim Lebanese. I had the greatest admiration for all the men at the sharp end, because they were always ready to help, to share their food and to talk freely, just as I remember the South Vietnamese soldiers did outside Quang Tri a decade ago. The very core of that admiration lies in the fact that as a reporter, I could always leave them when things got very bad. They stayed – as they have always stayed – and they never held it against me that I often left them.

To finish on a naïve, sentimental and moralizing note: some of the most dedicated, intelligent, honest and best-educated men in the Middle East are currently wasting their lives in Palestinian military camps all over the region, and there are a lot of shortsighted Arabs and Israelis who are happy they are stuck there. If those talents could be directed back to what they should be doing, as engineers and doctors and poets and teachers, they could create a state more dynamic than any other in the Middle East – which of course is the reason they frighten the daylights out of Arab and Israeli leaders.

I believe that Israel's only hope for the long-term future lies in the creation of a Palestinian state, on the West Bank and in Gaza to begin with. The Israelis say they can't have this because it would be a threat; 'a dagger at the heart of Israel' seems to be the popular way to describe it. Of course the opposite is exactly true, because it would be a weak little infant, entirely at the mercy of the people next door; a Palestine Liberation Organization whose offices were literally within cannon shot of Israel would be far more vulnerable and far less aggressive than one in Beirut or Tunis. If it comes to that, the thousands of fighters who have nothing to do now but plot vengeance would be too busy putting together their new world to have time to think of vengeance and – to be practical – they're going to be a lot more careful about risking their own state than they are about someone else's. I don't know if the plan would work, but proximity might give each side a chance to get to know the other as neighbours and give the Israelis a chance to integrate into the Middle East.

The alternative is yet more war, more Israeli pre-emptive strikes, more graves in martyrs' cemeteries from Beirut to Baghdad; and in the end, the state of Israel will be overrun. The Arabs have much more money, their numbers are increasing at a far greater rate and more importantly, even now the Israeli population is declining because nobody wants to go there. The Russian Jews who should be their main source of new blood, have heard all the stories already, so they head straight for America when they can escape from the *gulags*. It's not Arab will and skill that's going to overcome Israel if it doesn't change, but Arab money and numbers. The question has absolutely nothing to do with right or wrong: Israel will go because it has chosen to use the diplomacy of the gun to deal with its neighbours, and therefore they have no reason at all to want it to survive. I think this will happen in my lifetime – if I manage three score and ten – but if the Americans suddenly couldn't afford to pay for all their playthings, the whole thing could go in under five years.

The odd thing is that I can predict to a group of my liberal friends that South Africa will cease to exist because it has alienated and brutalized its neighbours, and because the whites are an island in a black sea; they all nod and say, 'Of course . . . well, naturally.' Yet when I say the same of Israel they say, 'No, it could never happen – the only democracy in the Middle East, biggest military power, previous victories, unthinkable.' Yet South Africa is far richer than Israel, its neighbours are infinitely poorer and worse equipped militarily and it's much more important to the West because it is more or less a solid block of gold and diamonds and platinum. In the end, states don't exist because they're decent or democratic, they exist because their neighbours let them, or they're too big and powerful to challenge. One day the Israelis will realize that Beirut 1982 was the time and the place where their myth of invincibility finally cracked. There are 13,000 men scattered throughout the Middle East now who are living proof of the end of that myth.

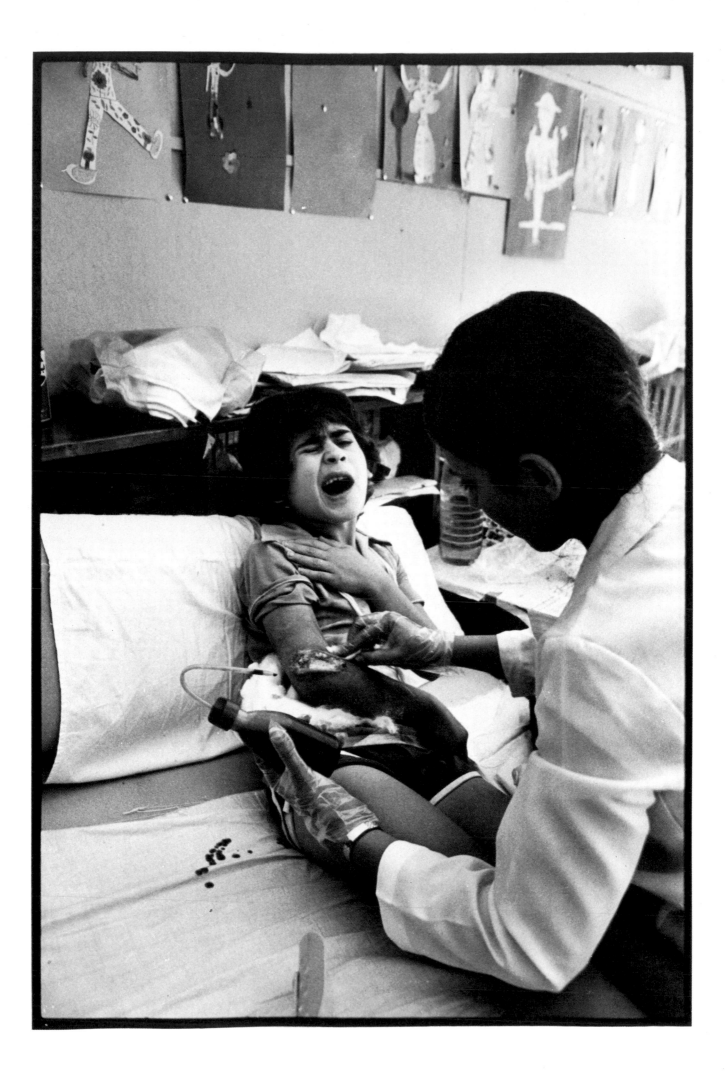

5
Prime Targets

'Well, son, you've graduated, you've got a good chemistry degree, you're a fine worker with a great future – what do you think you're going to do with your life?' Old Jack Mathews looked proudly at his son. He had worked hard for the boy and put in long hours of overtime in the steel mills so his son could have the best education money could buy; now here was John Jnr, fresh from the graduation ceremony, still in his gown, holding mortar and graduation scroll awkwardly in one hand, clinging to his mother's hand with the other. It was a high point in all their lives the old man thought, as they stood among the crowds of excited students and proudly smiling parents.

The boy hesitated, wondering how to express himself. It was something he had thought about for these past two years, the years when he realized he had the talents to become a really great scientist – not just a glorified bottle-washer and lab assistant, but an innovator, a man who could transmute ideas into reality. He had an honours degree of such quality that recruiters from industry were besieging him like scouts from the major leagues trying to sign the school's ace pitcher. 'Well, Dad,' he said hesitantly, almost shyly, 'I've given it a lot of thought. I've looked at the prospectuses, I've talked to the dean of the chemistry school, I've talked it over with all my friends. Dad,' he burst out excitedly, unable to hold back the secret any longer, 'I'm going into ordnance.'

Seeing the puzzled looks on the old people's faces, he felt he had to explain, the words tumbling over themselves as his innermost thoughts jostled for expression. 'See, I've been reading a lot about high-explosive shells, about mines and bombs and rockets, and I feel there's a lot I can contribute there. It's a field with real problems and challenges, Dad. I mean – well,

how do you get white phosphorus liquid enough so that it will really splash when the shells explode – not just in lumps, but soft so that it will spread all over a person's body? And how do you develop the sort of alloys that fracture into razor blades, so they really slash through kids' arms and legs? And bombs – Dad, I could think about bombs all day. Someone, and it could just be me, is going to work out one day how you get a bomb that will bore through eight floors of an apartment block and then explode, so the whole thing crunches up like a deck of cards. And cluster-bombs – they're so primitive now – I mean, half of those bomblets don't go off at all, and the rest of them are so under-powered they'll barely take a hand or a foot off. Dad, I tell you, there's a whole new world out there, and I mean to be part of it. It's my future, Dad!' Well, somebody must have thought like that you reflect, as you stand in the Gaza Hospital and look at what, on a backyard barbecue, would be a marvellous piece of T-bone. Dark brown and crackly on the surface, the deeper cracks showing the rare red meat underneath, the juices trickling down on the crisp sesame roll – sorry, on to the pillow – and in the middle of that juicy piece of protein a pair of eyes – pure Magritte, my dear. I do wish you could have seen it, complete with that little blue plug at the bottom to let the air get to the centre of the meat, but it went off, unfortunately, and just had to be thrown away after a couple of hours . . . such a waste. Plenty more, of course, but that one – just a touch of tabasco, maybe a little mayonnaise, and Craig Claiborne would have had it in colour in *The New York Times* magazine.

Some little Arthur or Carl-Heinz or Nathan or Kenzo or whoever probably spent a year or more working on that phosphorus problem. From my days at school, I seem to remember that it came in big hard yellow lumps and didn't spread at all. Someone with a Ph.D. in chemistry sat up all night worrying about Willie Pete and how you get it to spread like jello. No point in having a shell that explodes and just gives someone a headache when he gets whacked by a great hard lump of phosphorus – you've got to thin it out so it spreads like something Helena Rubenstein dreamed about: dragon-licks on your face and your arms and your tits and your balls, fizzing through your skin . . . the ultimate wrinkle-remover. Great thing about it, ordnance-wise, is that the bugger doesn't stop burning if you bandage it or throw water on it, or even so forget your dignity as to writhe in the dust: it just keeps burning and smoking away.

Not that you absolutely *had* to be barbecued – the nice thing about Beirut this time was that everyone was given a wide variety of choices: every day, something different. If you wanted a body that would have looked good as a rib joint, you stayed in your seaside apartment and waited for the navy to pump phosphorus shells in to the living-room – somehow, the navy more than anyone else seemed to have a real affection for that stuff. But if you wanted something a bit cleaner – more surgical, really – then it was better to hang around in the camps and wait for the tank rounds and the 155s to open up. Lot of shrapnel flying around to slit you open, rip your guts out, cut your throat – and you hardly felt it until you saw the looks on the faces of the ambulance guys picking you up: first a foot, then your body, put that leg in the plastic bag, maybe they can sew that chest up. There was even something for the kids: cluster-bombs, such fun things. Big grey-white bean-pods that opened up and threw these cute little golf balls all over the place. Kids just love playing with things like that . . . and they weren't all that harmful. I mean, they'll take your hands off and split your forearms open so they look like red orchids, and maybe little Abdul will come home slightly blinded, and there's always some klutz who'll kick one in the dark and ruin his chances of playing for Spurs; but basically those little balls gave kids the chance to participate, actually participate in a war, and still be around after-wards to tell *their* kids about what fun it all was. Looking back on it, that was the nice thing about the Beirut siege: the Israelis made it *everyone*'s siege; they spread the fun around so that, at the end of it, nobody in west Beirut could complain that he'd been left out of the action.

The big question was whether the Israelis really wanted to make everyone take part, or whether they were just spreading the joy around indiscriminately and hoping that everyone would get his or her chance to share in the excitement. We used to sit around all night in the Commodore debating the question: are they doing it all on purpose, or are they just spraying it around and hoping for the best? The crew led by Tom Friedman of *The New York Times*, said it was mainly just 'shoot an arrow into the air, it falls to earth I know not where' stuff. They actually argued that a lot of that shelling and bombing was indiscriminate (a word you can use around the bar of the Commodore with impunity, but not one you can get into *The New York Times*). The Friedman theory roughly went like this: it had to be indiscriminate because that incoming shit hit everything: hospitals, that Temple of Truth the Commodore Hotel, the apartment blocks full of middle-class Lebanese, movie theatres, even the Magen Abraham synagogue. It squashed middle-class Christians in their big apartments in Ramlet al-Baida; it blew the legs off Kurdish cigarette salesmen in Hamra; it burned the faces off teenage girls in Sabra camp and minced old men playing back-gammon in their antiques shops in Basta. The theory that the Israeli soldiers manning the Ring of Steel round west Beirut didn't care what they hit was one supported by probably eighty per cent of the hacks; but the others said those guys knew exactly what they were doing, and if they blew the feet off some seventy-year-old woman silly enough to be crossing an open road on the way to the bakery, it was because they wanted to drive the shoemakers out of business, and luck had nothing to do with it.

There was no question but that the Israelis could hit anything they wanted to when they were really trying. Five times they flattened buildings just after Arafat had been in or near them. He'd appear in one of his little convoys; twenty minutes later, a couple of F-16s would appear out of nowhere, plunge down like sharks, 'wallop', then away, leaving the great red cloud of dust rising like blood in still water and the building they had just whacked collapsing in a rain of broken glass and concrete. If they wanted an apartment block or a hotel or one of the Palestinians' tired old tanks, they just came and got it: flip by in air-conditioned comfort; no need to hurry, no need to worry about the silly little Sam-7 rounds falling 5,000 feet short; no need to do all that Second World War stuff like getting targets in cross-wires and braving the ack-ack to get on target. Let the computers do the thinking, head in the general direction of the target, press the button when told to, then get back to base in time to meet the press corps and announce another successful mission against the terrorists. Everything wire-guided, electronically steered, computer-controlled, laser-directed. Sit in your cockpit or your tank turret or your cabin, eat a *knish* with one hand and press the red button with the other. After you spent a few days watching what looked like dog dinners being dug out of totally squashed buildings, you did believe they could hit anything. They were sometimes so accurate you wondered if they really have a smart bomb tuned to the wavelengths given off by short Arab leaders with inch-long stubble on their chins – perhaps they didn't; but remember the time the man was seen near the big apartment block near Sanayeh Gardens, and twenty minutes later they put an air-strike in that was so accurate it ripped the guts out of the whole building without even breaking the glass in the windows of the block fifteen yards across the road.

Yes, well all right, there were times the Israelis were so uncannily on target that you got to believe they could knock a fly off a steak lying on a plate at the Commodore from 7,000 yards with a Gabriel missile . . . But in that case, if they *could* just knock out military targets, why did they keep hitting hospitals? When the siege started, there were seventeen hospitals in west Beirut; by the time the fighting finished, five were closed and one had been badly damaged by bombs and shells; and the Barbir Hospital, a major centre for treating civilian wounded, took at least a dozen hits. It got to the point where it seemed, not that the Israelis were trying to miss the hospitals, but that they had been made prime targets. Claire Constant, a French nurse from an aid organization called *Médecins sans Frontières* (a sort of flying squad of doctors and nurses who rush around the world from one hell-hole to another), said that when her team established their makeshift hospital in the sub-basement of an underground car-park in Bourj Barajneh, they deliberately didn't hang the traditional Red Cross flags about the place 'because we didn't want to attract the attention of the Israeli gunners and pilots'.

Perhaps if you were someone like Ariel Sharon you could torture facts far enough to make the excuse that you had to hit a hospital like the Barbir because they did take in wounded fighters from time to time, and after all the war was supposed to be about eliminating 'terrorists' . . . A hard decision to take, blowing up a hospital full of wounded women and kids to get a couple of terrorists, but defence ministers can't be sentimentalists. All right, Ariel, we'll allow you Barbir for the time being, but did you have to hit the hospital for the mentally handicapped in Sabra? And not hit it once, which could have been an accident, but at least five times (I didn't get a chance to go back after the fifth hit). Five times . . . Was it belted so often because the euthanasia lobby in the Defence Department thought it kinder to put those 850 starving lunatics out of their misery before they drowned in their own shit? Or was it because Mossad had convinced you that those twisted kids, covered in purple bedsores, were really artfully disguised 'terrorists', just waiting to take the 'Peace' out of Operation Peace For Galilee?

I got to the hospital for the mentally disabled by taking

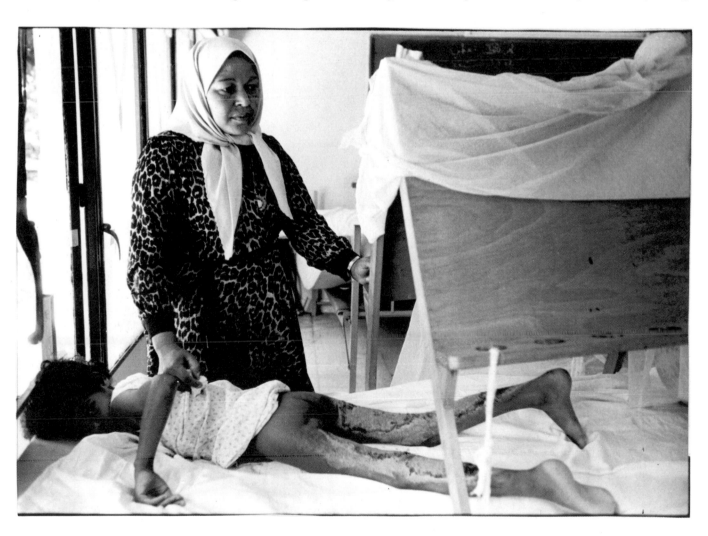

a right turn off the rubble-clogged main shopping street at the beginning of the Sabra camp and following the winding passageways (I wouldn't call them streets) up to the hospital, near the edge of the sports stadium – once a modern concrete amphitheatre, now a collapsed dish of broken fragments of walls and benches – a sort of instant Colosseum. The hospital was one of those totally unmemorable modern hospitals that could just as easily be a biscuit factory or a technical school: rectangular, five floors, rows of rectangular windows with a short flight of concrete steps up to the entrance; and not too badly damaged from the outside: just a bit chipped, like a kid's playhouse with the edges and more fragile bits broken off by being thumped around a little. There was a small admissions office by the wrought-iron front gates, but that was deserted and all its glass long since blown out, and there were fresh shrapnel tears in the wood-work. Standing by that office entrance, I had no reason to suspect that any part of the place was inhabited; there was none of the life I associate with hospitals: no nurses running around, no ambulances, no officious porters asking why you want to come in, no anxious relatives; none of the street vendors you normally see outside Middle Eastern hospitals: the people who pile magazines and soap and bananas and matches and medicines all along the pavements. So deserted that if I hadn't been told about it, I wouldn't have bothered to go past the front gate – after all, this was one of the most dangerous parts of Beirut, this was terrorist country – and the Israelis had belted it from land and sea every day of the siege (air attacks were special treats that only came about three times a week to minimize the strain on the poor pilots).

I walked up the chipped, deserted steps and into the front hall, a dark cube which probably never looked much better than a prison reception area, even when there had been a power supply to light it. I shouted silly things like 'Anyone home?' and eventually a small girl dressed like a nurse but perhaps only fifteen appeared from a darkened corridor; she took me by the hand to the stairs and gestured upwards. At the top of the stairs was a man in a white coat – a doctor, the medical director maybe, I assumed, because this was after all one of the biggest hospitals in Lebanon. He was a Palestinian orderly, Ahmed Mohammed Sabha; come to that, he was the medical director, as well as chief psychiatrist, physiotherapist, dietician. In fact all the qualified staff had long gone – some too terrified to stay, some needed more urgently in hospitals dealing with war-wounded. Ahmed Mohammed Sabha was now the head man; he had a staff of maybe six trained nurses to look after hundreds. This was a case of the mad caring for the mad, because the rest of the auxiliaries were the saner of the mental cripples caught in this concrete trap.

Ahmed Sabha has had journalists in before. I should go to the top of the building and work downwards, he says. He gave me the statistics as we climbed to the top

floor. Male mental patients: 140; senile patients: 400, mainly old men; the rest spastic and mentally defective children of both sexes aged from about five to eighteen. Yes, many of them were Palestinians and probably had relatives in the camps, but they had been driven away by the bombing. They were funded by the Lebanese government, but they hadn't had any money for a month; there wasn't any food and hadn't been for a week, apart from what the staff could beg or buy with their own money. The hospital had been hit five times so far. This was the children's ward, here on the top floor where the sun can shine in through the big windows. There was a vast splash of orange across the whole of one wall where the phosphorus shell had exploded – a week after the hit, your fingers still burn if you touch the stain. There were pictures on the wall: koalas, kittens, puppies. The cots were covered with dust and pieces of glass and some had been charred by the phosphorus flames. The other half of the floor was a dining-room; this was where the six old men had been killed when another shell crashed into the building at lunch-time. From the fifth floor I could see the damage the bombing had done to the stadium outside: a vista of ruins that could be a thousand years old with the ruined stadium at its heart. I was reminded of the quality of Israeli fire-power by the sight of a Mercedes lying upside down like a stranded tortoise on the roof of the two-storey house immediately below me. There was no sign of human life as far as the eye could see.

The human life was shuffling in the corridors below. These were never especially violent people and the continual sound of shelling, instead of making them more fearful or more crazed, as it might do to normal people, had quietened them down: they crept around the corridors as if they believed that by not making a noise they would manage not to attract the attention of the monsters that were outside battering on their walls. They had long since learned that the exposed wards were dangerous, and most huddled in the corridors or shuffled along close to the walls, muttering to them-selves, a few talking quietly. On the fourth floor were the women and girls, the more lucid ones in shapeless floral dresses, a few in dressing-gowns, the quiet mad ones sitting bolt upright and naked on the floor, staring straight ahead. Not all the wards were empty; in some, totally catatonic women lay, silent, staring up at the ceilings, fists and jaws clenched, flies crawling into the corners of their eyes. A girl with a shaven head tugged at my arm: 'My name is Samira abu Zaki, my name is Samira abu Zaki,' she said in French. 'My father is Yousef abu Zaki, you must get a message to him. You must tell him I am here, you must tell him that he has to come and take me away.' The women around her nodded to each other, whispered and pointed at me. 'My name is Samira abu Zaki, you must tell my father to take me away from here.'

When you write about things like this, you try, and

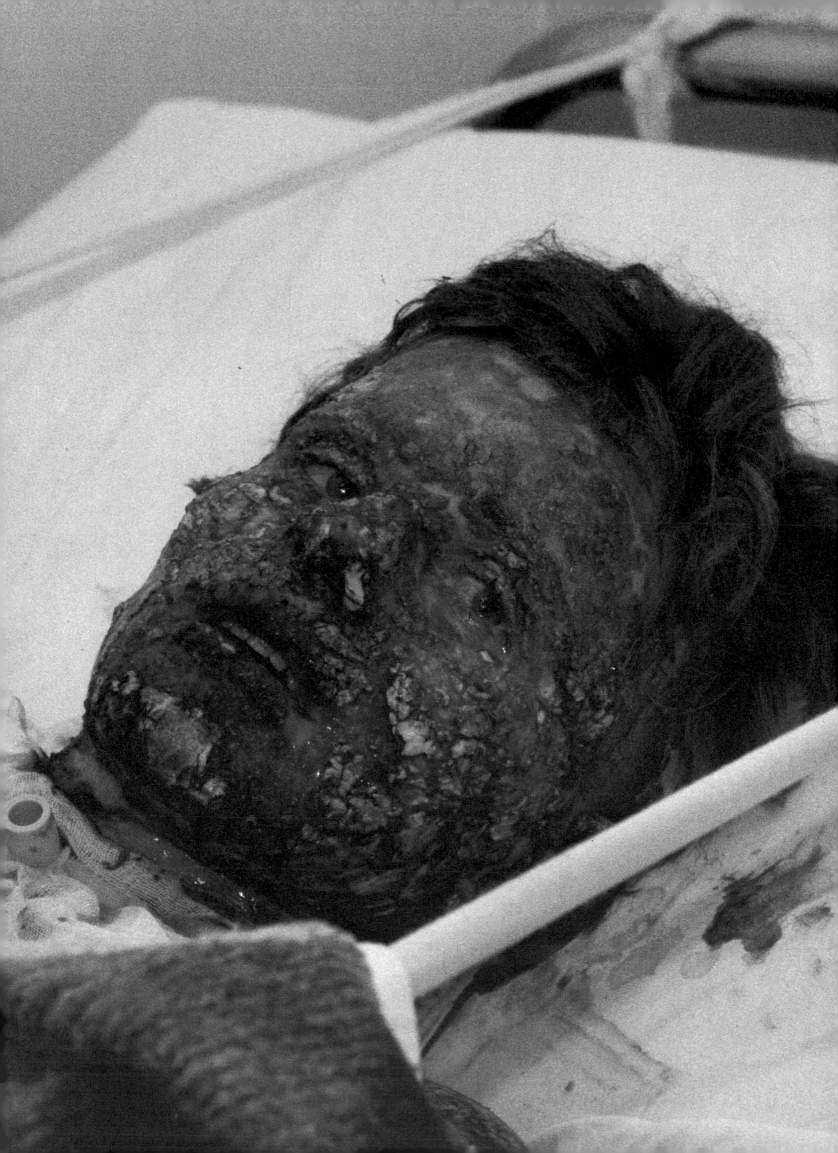

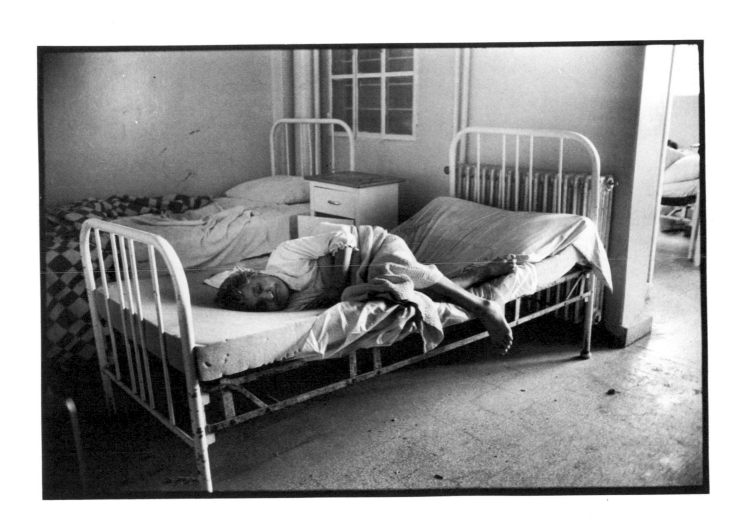

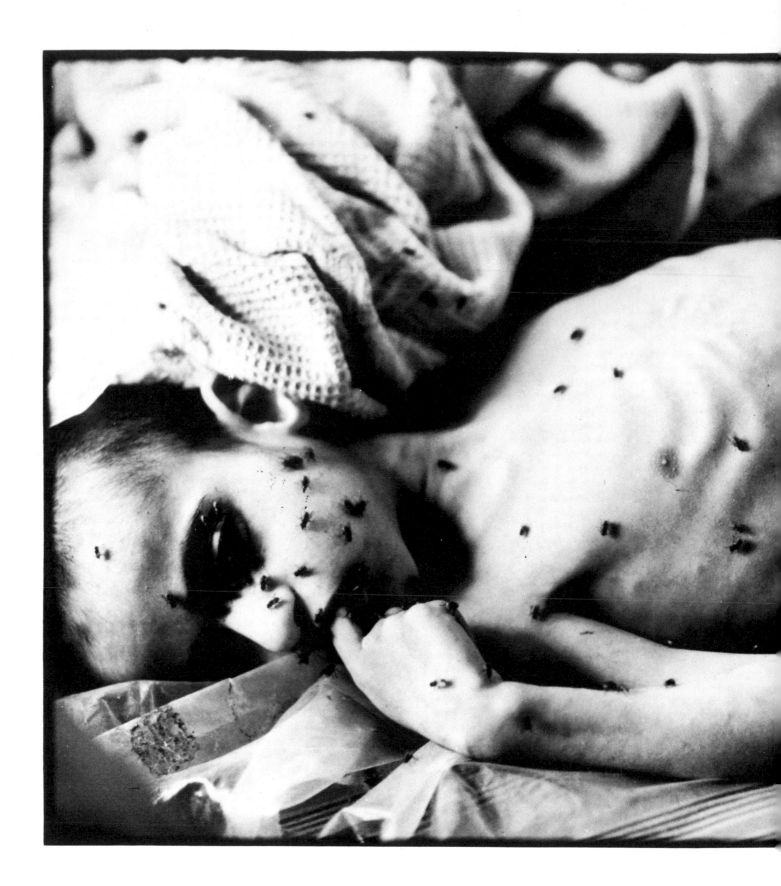

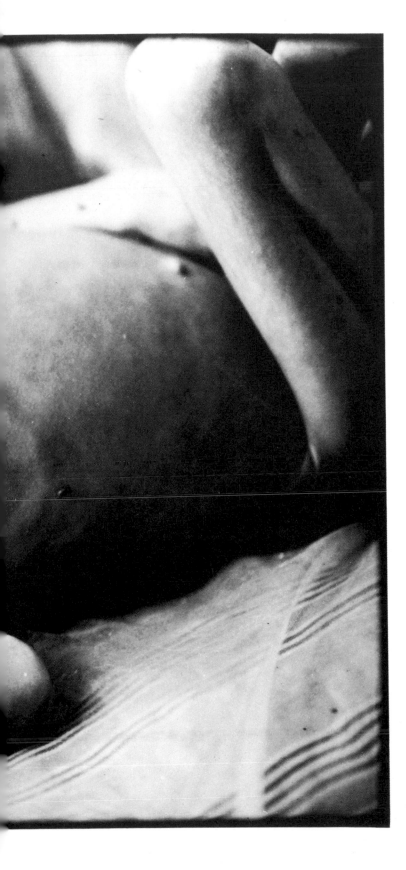

then you fail to avoid saying things like 'descending the stairs of the hospital for the mentally disabled in Beirut was like descending into Dante's inferno'. The deeper you went, the worse it got. None of the old men on the next floor was strong enough or had wit enough to look after anyone but himself, so the bedridden were never wakened, the very weak were never fed. The tiny staff were trying to save the very young, so the old men were simply left to themselves.

'What are they saying?' I asked Ahmed Sabha as the old men in long striped flannel nightgowns clustered around us, gently pulling at our arms, whispering in our ears.

'They are saying they want to eat, they have not eaten for four days. They are saying "food, food" and "eat, eat".'

Through a doorway, two corpses lay on their beds – they had been there for two days. A third, equally corpselike figure lay on the third bed; Ahmed Sabha rolled open an eyelid in the gaunt yellow face; the pupil still reacted to light. 'Tomorrow,' he said, closing the eyelid.

Journalists always go to hospitals in war zones; all that is pathetic, all that is pitiable, all that sums up the futility and hatefulness of war is concentrated in a hundred bloodstained beds. You want widows, you want limbless children, you want men with their balls blown off, you want beautiful girls with no faces, you want tears and screams and the sort of great pictures that editors don't want to print because it reminds the folks back home that wars can play hell with the most carefully applied make-up – you go to the nearest hospital and start clicking and writing away, and nobody there is going to refuse to talk or tell you to piss off because probably they can't open their mouths anyway, and those who can probably have only a stump to threaten you with. In Beirut, everyone went to hospitals; looking back on it, if I could recapture two minutes of time to show Menachem Begin what Operation Peace For Galilee came to mean, I would use those two minutes to take him on a tour of the children's wards of the hospital for the mentally disabled.

What would I start with? Maybe that inner room in the heart of the building which had no windows and so was safe from the bombing. I opened the door and the piss which had been dammed up behind the door literally ran out over my shoes. The piss was from the thirty or forty naked children, maybe three to five years old, squatting along the walls. The ammonia stink was so heavy I had to hold my breath, it made my eyes water; and I took a couple of minutes to make out the little pot-bellied shapes crouching in the darkness. Potential terrorists, of course – the problem with the Palestinians is that they keep on breeding, no matter how hard you bomb them, and by Christ the old hospital for the mentally disabled got bombed often enough.

Give that reeking incubator one minute, then use the

other minute to lead Mr Begin across the hallway and into one of the wards with the spastics in it. It's true they're exposed to danger there; the floor is covered with broken glass – but there's kind of a problem with spastics, you see. There are about three or four of them on each foam-mattress, and because they're all twisted up by their diseases, and because they tend to writhe about a bit when the stale urine soaked into the mattresses hits their open bedsores, they sort of get, well, 'tangled' is the best word. So, if you try to pick up one of these twisted fifty-pound skeletons, the others tend to come with it, like those rows of paper figures you used to cut out of newspapers when you were a kid. There must have been about twenty bundles of them, maybe sixty kids in all, probably any ages from about eight to fifteen. If you wanted to unwind a few and turn them the right way up, you could usually find out what sex they were; they were all naked but, what with their heads being shaved and their appendages being pretty shrunken by starvation, it was not as easy a task as telling the bodyguards from the entrants at the 'Miss World' contest. They couldn't talk, either – which made separating the Fatimas from the Abduls even more difficult.

I went to that hospital three times to chart its miserable history. I was there in the morning and in the afternoon, and I wandered around the area to see if I could find parents or family or anyone who knew any of the patients. At the end of the first month of the war, it was one of the few inhabited buildings in the whole area – that part of town had been half flattened by some of the most concentrated shelling and bombing of the war. It was not surrounded by military positions; it was not a base for guerrillas; it was not an ammunition dump; it had no guns on its roof; the military and most civilians had long since decided the area was just too dangerous and had left it there in the middle of the wasteland . . . yet it was hit again and again by Israeli shelling, mostly from the sea, by those deadly accurate little gunboats whose guns (we were told) are electronically controlled so that even if the ship rolls, the gun stays on target. Stay on target they certainly did: the building was raked from top to bottom, phosphorus in the top floors, high-explosive in the middle, some sort of fragmentation shell in the courtyard that ripped open the fragile wooden outbuildings.

It's almost a cliché because ambulance drivers and doctors and nurses working in war zones have been written about before, but the bravest people in Beirut during the war were the ones who worked in the hospitals. The reports show that the places themselves were dangerous because they were hit repeatedly by shelling and bombing throughout the war.

Q.: 'But surely, Mr Clifton, you're not suggesting that the Israeli armed forces deliberately shelled and bombed hospitals?'

A.: 'That's exactly what I'm saying. Too many got hit too often for them just to have been lucky.'

The hospitals were not only dangerous; because many of them were near the perimeters where the fighting was fiercest, it was usually a hair-raising experience just to get to one. You'd creep down towards the Acca Hospital on the edge of Chatila or down to the mental hospital in Sabra or to Claire Constant's underground emporium

and by the time you got there you'd feel like jumping into the nearest bed and calling for the largest dose of Valium in the house.

Claire Constant, like Catherine Leroy, was a totally insane French woman who seemed to have spent most of her time trying to get herself blown into orbit by one set of baddies or another. She had done three tours in Afghanistan with medical teams working with the guerrillas before she came to Beirut; she flies helicopters and small planes in her spare time; in Beirut, she not only worked in the hospital – which was hairy enough – but regularly went out with the ambulance teams looking for

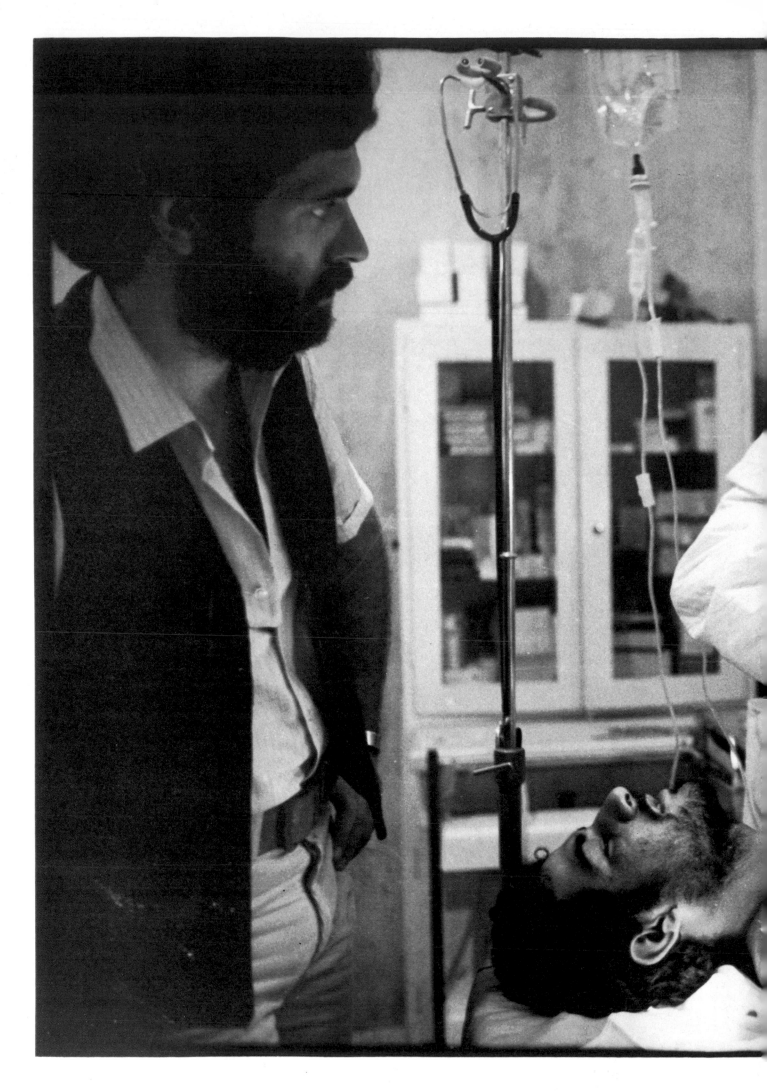

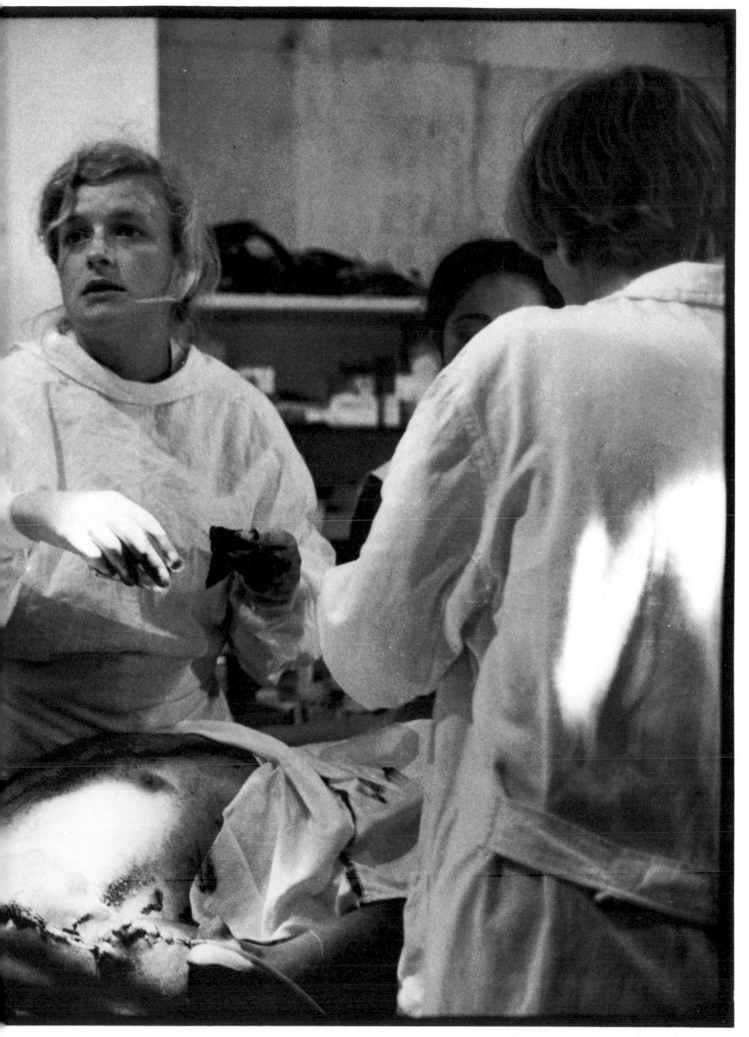

'There were times when I felt I was working in a horror movie' – Claire Constant, *Médecins sans Frontières*

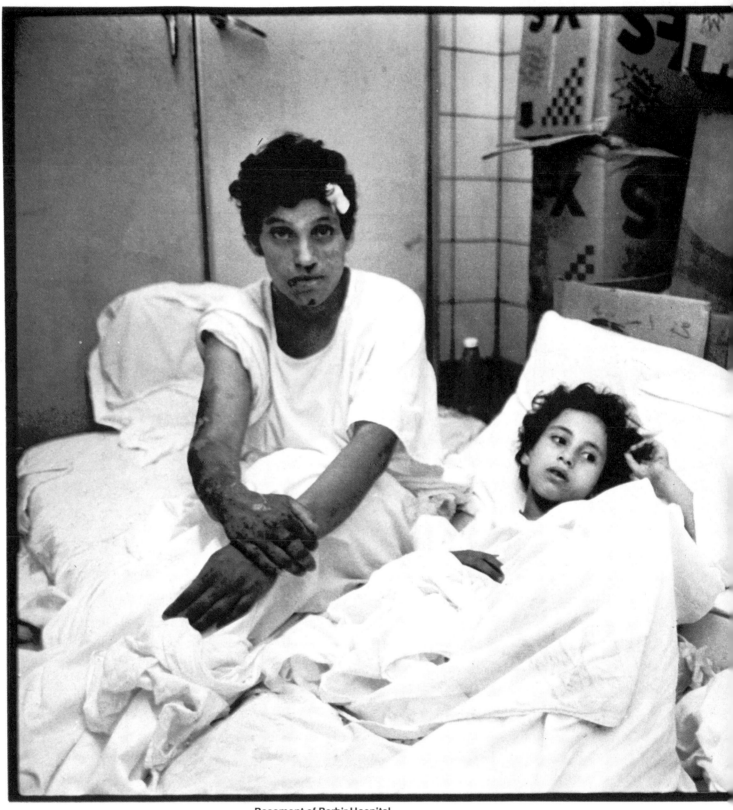

Basement of Barbir Hospital

patients. This was the most dangerous job of all: the way you got your customers in those days was to jump in your ambulance and head into the heart of the worst shelling and bombing, because you knew that that was where the people who most needed you would be lying.

She was interviewed for a story on *Médecins sans Frontières* after the war; she described what it was like

driving into 'the mushrooms of black and white smoke'. The ambulance buckets across the shell craters to the scene of a bombing attack near Bourj Barajneh; the clouds of smoke and flame are so intense they can hardly see what they are doing. 'We rush into the ruins, around us there is a wave of hysteria. Women scream and cry, beating their heads with both hands and falling to their

with shrapnel. I take the child like a sleep-walker and get into the vehicle. To make room for us, Ali, one of the ambulance attendants, gets out and clings to the outside of the door as we rush back. The little boy is already breathing with difficulty and I clasp him tightly to me saying, "He must last until we get to the hospital." '

In fact the child died on the way. The ambulance was shelled a few minutes later; Ali had his foot slashed off by splinters; more hit the child in Claire's arms, and it bled to death before they got it to safety. She ended her interview by saying, 'Those shells were meant for me.'

I would see Claire in the hotel, having a drink with Catherine one night; another, we'd all drink a lot of champagne to celebrate Catherine's birthday. Then Claire would disappear for days, and I might see her next, if it was a very quiet day, swimming off the rocks under the ruined fish-restaurants at Raouche. She worked with a team of foreign doctors and nurses, but most of the non-technical help came from local kids, boys of fifteen and sixteen who wanted desperately to be fighters, but had been turned down by the militia because of their age. So they had come round to the hospital to volunteer as drivers and aides and stretcher-bearers – 'stretcher-bearers' is probably the wrong word because they didn't have any stretchers, so they would use an old chair and carry people out of the rubble and to the ambulance with that. 'Until the war came, they'd never done anything brave in their lives – or had any chance to do anything useful either, if it came to that,' Claire said of her helpers. 'They came from poor families, they hadn't had jobs and had spent half their lives sitting around pinball parlours, smoking cigarettes and playing the machines. But they were oblivious to danger and would go anywhere, no matter whether they were under fire or not. They would never turn back. They were always asking what else they could do to help, and one day we said that our worst problem was that we never had enough blood for the wounded. They didn't understand what we were saying at first, but then we explained that they could give blood. Whenever we ran short they would immediately volunteer, and they would sometimes give blood twice a day or for several days in a row. Then you'd be out working with one; he'd suddenly fall over, unconscious, at your feet, and you'd realize he'd keeled over because he'd been giving so much blood.'

You have to be very tough, mentally and physically, to do the sort of job Claire and people like her did. You have to be very brave to work under fire; you have to be physically tough to work very long hours under stress, and you have to be mentally tough to withstand the horrors around you. It was not easy to be a reporter in Beirut, but we could always leave an area if the action got too heavy and more than anything, we rarely got physically involved in what we were doing. By that I mean, although we might go through fire to the scene of a bombing, like Claire, we did not then actually have to

knees. Some unharmed children, wild-eyed and dumb with horror, run barefoot in the rubble looking for their families; one of them is a girl of about six, scrabbling in the ruins, lifting up the debris around her. Then the ambulance starts to move, loaded with wounded. As we pull away, a man runs up to me, his eyes clouded with tears. He holds out his small son to me, the boy is riddled carry the bleeding, screaming people out of the ruins and back to the hospital, to work on keeping them alive. I would take notes about what I had seen then go back to the hotel to a clean room, a beer and a typewriter to record it all. Claire would load someone into the ambulance, hold them together as they bounced through the shell-pitted streets, and then probably follow them into the operating theatre. If Catherine had taken a picture of me at work, she would probably have caught me on the outskirts of some disaster or other, taking notes and not getting involved in the turmoil in front of me. When she took a picture of Claire, she caught her in the operating room, standing over an unconscious man who looks as if someone had tried to cut him in half, both longitudinally and horizontally. There he lies, with Claire poised above him: tubes running into his head, his arm and shoulder split from neck to elbow and held together by half a yard of stitching. *I* could walk away, having done my job just by being there and noting what happened. When I was leaving, people like Claire and the ambulance men were only beginning. I would see a wounded man for two minutes, then he'd be gone; Claire would probably stay with him until he recovered or, just as likely, died.

'There were times when I felt I was working in a horror movie,' she told Catherine. 'They'd bring in someone who'd been in a building hit by a phosphorus shell, and you'd start to take his clothes off, and his skin would come off with the clothes. We'd have children brought in with their bellies split open by shrapnel, and others with their brains leaking out of holes in their heads. I remember one day they brought in a teenage boy and I helped him out of the chair he was being carried in and down the steps. His face was drenched in blood because the shrapnel had ripped open his face and torn his eyes out. He heard me talk and he turned and smiled at me and said, "I want you to wash this blood out of my eyes so I can see what you look like." He didn't know it, but I was helping him take his first steps as a blind man.

'By the time we reached the end of the war, the laundry at our hospital had packed up, so we couldn't get any clean clothes. At the end, we were all working in clothes that creaked because they were completely saturated with dried blood. When I left Beirut I felt as if I was leaving hell.'

I think most of us reporters did fairly regular hospital rounds, checking casualty figures, doing stories on the doctors and nurses, trying to find out what the Israeli horror weapon of the week was. After a couple of weeks, you couldn't help but notice that there seemed to be new holes in half the hospitals you visited; by the end of a month you didn't so much wonder whether they were being hit on purpose – you accepted that as obvious – you wondered more whether there was some kind of battery that did nothing but hit hospitals. I mean, when the Israeli reconnaissance planes came back with the high-resolution photographs of Beirut which would clearly have shown the big red crosses on the tops of the hospitals, was some group of ace gunners detailed to go and blow them to bits? Were they told that in the Arab world, red crosses were always painted on the roofs of ammunition dumps; or did some bluff old colonel get them all together and give them a pep talk on the value of knocking out the places? 'After all, chaps, what you have to remember, as the P.M. says, is that they're all terrorists down there. Give him time and that terrorist who's flat on his back in the Barbir now is going to get well, and before you know it he'll be back rocketing Galilee. You can't be sentimental about these chaps, better get them before they get you.' Who knows, someone in the Israeli Defence Ministry might even now be compiling a manual based on the experiences of 1982, perhaps a booklet on the lines of *A soldier's guide to modern hospital destruction*. The introduction would emphasize, of course, that it was important for public-relations reasons not to flatten the place with a 1,000-pounder. The object in knocking out a hospital was to leave it standing, so the press wouldn't get too excited, but to hit it often enough with relatively small-calibre ordnance to terrify the staff, kill a selection of the patients and so disrupt its water, power and medical supplies that it could never be much more than the charnel house that the hospital for the mentally retarded so satisfyingly became.

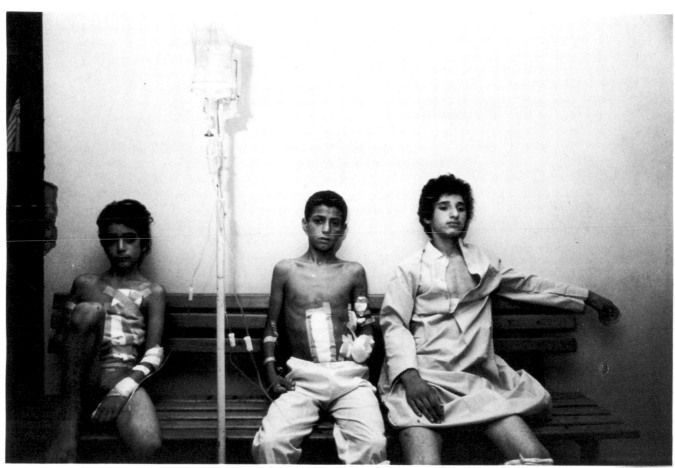

Gaza Hospital

Tal Zaatar, August 1976

The survivors

6
Tal Zaatar, 1976

When you get to the heart of this chapter, you might begin to wonder what it is doing in a book about the siege of Beirut by the Israelis in 1982, because what you will be reading is an interview with a Palestinian woman living in Baghdad and talking about a massacre that happened six years before the Israeli army got to Beirut. The reason I wanted Randa Ibrahim al Dhoukhi to tell the story of the siege of Tal Zaatar and the massacre of her people by Christian gunmen after the camp fell is that to know why the Palestinians fought so well in Beirut, you have to know about Tal Zaatar first. If there had been no Tal Zaatar, it is just conceivable that the Palestinians' will to fight to the death might have weakened under the savagery of the bombardment. In the end they were not defeated; they held their line for a number of reasons, among them national pride and personal bravery; but they also knew what would happen if the Israelis managed to break open their defences and unleashed their Christian allies on west Beirut. Tal Zaatar was where the Palestinians learnt that the Christian militia had the deepest hatred for them, a hatred that fuelled the worst massacre Lebanon has seen since the civil war began in 1975 and, in terms of people killed, worse even than Sabra or Chatila in 1982.

Until 1975, the Palestinians in the Tal Zaatar camp had lived peacefully among their Christian neighbours on a sloping hillside in east Beirut, overlooking the sea. Like the Jews who stayed behind in Eastern Europe until it was too late, the people of Tal Zaatar misread the omens when the Lebanese civil war broke out in 1975. Instead of getting out when they had the chance, while it was still possible for a person with a Palestinian accent to drive through east Beirut to the west, they stayed among the people they had known all their lives. I imagine that like the Jews in Europe in the 1930s, some of them

couldn't believe they could be mistreated by people they had lived among for almost thirty years; others stayed because their homes and possessions were in Tal Zaatar and they couldn't afford to move, or they just didn't want to go somewhere else. Tal Zaatar was surrounded on 22 June 1976; it fell fifty-two days and seventy major assaults later, on 12 August. More than 2,500 of the people who were trapped in the camp died, either during the siege or in the blood-bath that followed when the Christian forces finally broke through the last cordon of starving defenders. Men, women and children were butchered without mercy, the bare ground was covered with slimy mud made of a mixture of human blood and red dust. Today, the central camp area on the extreme south-east edge of the city is a bare patch of land in a crowded Christian suburban area – from half a mile away it looks like an overgrown stone quarry; only when you get up close to it do you realize that what from a distance look like rock outcrops are actually the partly overgrown remains of dynamited concrete houses. Fig trees grow through the cracks in flattened walls, lizards bask on what were once flat roofs, and here and there you can still find the skeletons of broken furniture and disintegrating strips of discarded clothing. Tal Zaatar has ceased to exist as a place of human habitation; it is a deserted wasteland. But it lives on in the minds of every Palestinian trapped in Beirut in 1982. They had all heard the stories of survivors of Tal Zaatar, people like Randa Ibrahim al Dhoukhi; they all knew what to expect if the Israelis were allowed to break into west Beirut. It is no exaggeration to say that Tal Zaatar was one of the main reasons why Israel didn't take west Beirut in 1982.

'The terrorist had said little while his mother told the story of the most harrowing days of her life

– unemotionally he listened to her story of starvation and murder, of the death of his grandfather and great grandfather, of the way his uncle had been carried off by gunmen and never seen again. It was a tale that made little impression on him; in fact, as the horrors mounted, he became less and less interested and his head started to nod. Perhaps he had heard it all before, perhaps his nature was such that tales of human misery meant nothing to him. Finally he fell asleep; his mother picked him up in her arms and curled him on the sofa where he slept. It had been a long day for a boy of two.'

Now there's a good news-magazine introduction: lead the reader gently into the story, suggest the terrible things to come, then belt him with the bit about the 'terrorist' being only two. Shock him into reading on; see if you can grab him by the throat so hard for the first couple of lines that he'll read on to the finish. Get him interested by a little journalistic flim-flam, then let the real person tell the story.

This is the story of Randa Ibrahim al Dhoukhi, whose life-story to date has been such that I would have expected to have to talk to her in a padded cell while they pumped the tranquillizers into her with a fire-extinguisher. Her odyssey hasn't finished yet – and Christ knows where she'll end up – but what follows is how she tells it. You wouldn't have to do much scene-

Randa

Phalangist gunners outside Tal Zaatar

88

shifting or name-changing to shift Randa into the Warsaw ghetto in the Second World War. As it is, this story is about what happened in Tal Zaatar in 1976.

They always used to say that the civil war in Beirut was the war between the Well of the Pomegranate and the Hill of Thyme. The Well of the Pomegranate was Ain Rummaneh, a Christian suburb in south Beirut that was like a tongue lapping out into the Muslim suburbs to its west (*ain* is 'well' in Arabic, *rummaneh* is 'pomegranate'). Ain Rummaneh was hammered throughout the three years of the civil war – I remember being with a Lebanese leftist militia group one night in 1976 in the neighbouring suburb of Chiyah and watching them spray heavy anti-aircraft shells into the Ain Rummaneh buildings all night. I'm not sure where we were, although I have a feeling we might have been in a ruined church; but I do remember asking one of the fighters I was with what the Arabic slogan scrawled on the wall above our heads read, and he said it read, 'Abu Gdab lives here'. I asked who Abu Gdab was; after they found someone with better English, he explained he was 'the father of wrath'. It was pretty much the sort of place you would expect to find Abu Gdab. From where we were, if we had been able to drive a tank through the crumbling concrete walls of Ain Rummaneh ahead of us and headed due east for about a mile and a half, we would have come to the foot of the Hill of Thyme (*tal* is Arabic for 'hill' and *zaatar* is the aromatic wild thyme Palestinians brew into the tea they offer you whenever you have talked to them for two minutes). Tal Zaatar was a Palestinian refugee-camp set up in the purely Christian areas of east Beirut in 1948 when the first Palestinians had been driven out of Palestine and were welcomed as refugees throughout the Middle East, in those long-gone days when nobody asked an Arab refugee what his religion was before he was offered a cup of tea and somewhere to live. So when the civil war started in 1975, the Palestinians in Tal Zaatar suddenly found themselves entirely surrounded by Christian suburbs where they had very few friends.

We met Randa during a visit to Baghdad late in 1982. We had gone to see some Palestinian friends, and one of them said we should talk to Randa al Dhoukhi, because her life-story had made his hair stand on end – and he was a man who had had his friends blown up by letter-bombs and squashed flat in their houses, and had generally been given the sort of hard time that Palestinians get when they decide to become guerrillas.

The day I talked to her, Randa would have passed for the secretary of some successful Arab import/export company. She was wearing a navy-blue suit with a navy-blue waistcoat, and a sensible pale blue-grey cotton shirt; I remember she had light blue-grey stockings that had spots of mud on them, because the first of the winter rains had arrived just as she was coming up the road to meet us. She was leading the terrorist by the hand; he was wearing blue corduroy overalls, a white jumper and

the sort of leather cap with ear-flaps and fur on the inside that someone like the Bulgarians issued to the Palestinian guerrillas as part of their winter kit. Randa sat down on a black plastic armchair and started to tell her story, and the terrorist first lay on her lap and played with her bangles, then he started to nod off and went to sleep, and then she picked him up and laid him, half curled up, on a sofa while she told us the story of her life, in Arabic which our friend translated. She never cried while she was talking, but there were parts of her story when her clear voice became much louder and more penetrating, and other times when she completely ignored the interpreter and rushed on as if she feared that, if she stopped, she would never be able to start again. She talked for longer than four hours, and she began at the beginning – which, for every Palestinian I think I have ever met, is to tell you what part of Palestine her family came from.

'My name is Randa Ibrahim al Dhoukhi and I am twenty. My father came from Farad, which is a village north of Acre in Palestine, in 1948. First he lived in the Chouf Mountains in Lebanon, and then in 1959 he took my mother to Tal Zaatar. I was born there and so were my two sisters and three of my brothers. My fourth brother was born in 1976 after my father had been killed in Tal Zaatar.

'It was very bad there you know. At the beginning, we would get a little food and water, and some medicine would be allowed in; but that did not last very long. From the beginning to the end we hoped, we hoped that, maybe tomorrow, help would come. Sometimes someone would manage to get out, but they never returned and even today I have never met anyone who left the camp from those days.

'The worst problem of all was water. There was only one well that we could reach, and there were many battles fought for it. Sometimes the Phalangists would take it, and then our fighters would take it back. Even when we held it there would be snipers, and many people were killed trying to get water. We used to say that in those days one glass of water cost one glass of blood. There was one time when the Phalangists held the well for thirteen days and some of the babies died because there was no water. Our fighters took it back but the snipers were there, and some of the people who were shot fell into the well. I remember that after many days when we got to the well, we lowered our buckets into it and the buckets came up with blood in the water and fingernails at the bottom of the bucket. We would boil the water and then drink it because there wasn't any other. One day, nineteen days before my aunt was due to give birth, she went to the well and a rocket was fired and she was killed with thirteen others. We got the body back, but one hour later the Phalangists took the well again.

'I was fourteen years old. I used to help make food for our fighters and bandage their wounds and I would take my turn to go to the well. One day we were drawing water. There was a crowd of us and I was at the front putting my bucket in the well when a rocket fell and killed the people standing behind me. One of them was my best friend, Aisha al Jailouni. I was hit in the head by a piece of shrapnel and I remember that although it was a hot day my blood felt cold as it dried on my back. Just after that rocket fell, the Phalangists charged the well and we all had to run. I had to leave Aisha behind and I never saw her again. At that time we had no medicine for our wounds, just salt and water, and, when I washed my head-wound with it, my hair fell out. Before that time I had long thick hair, now it is very thin and still will not grow long.

back, my uncle saw the fighters with a wounded man and ran out to them and said, "Put him on my back, I'll carry him." He did not know the fighter was his son. Then he came to our shelter and laid my cousin on the ground and he saw that it was his son. He tried to talk to him, but my cousin died, and as he died my uncle's other son came in and he had been shot through the leg.

'Every day, another building would collapse because of the shelling and those of us who were still alive would have to move into the buildings that were left. On the last night, the fighters got through to Yasser Arafat on the radio and asked what they should do. He said, "Don't surrender." Then the fighters came back from the edges of the camp to say goodbye to us. They said

Crossing to safety, August 1976

'The camp was the most important place in the world for us. Near the end, the Phalangists had taken the top of the hill above us and had raised their flag there. My cousin Mohammed said, "I'll get it," and he and some friends fought their way up the hill and he climbed the pole to pull it down. He was shot in the chest and one of his friends laid him on a long piece of board and started to carry him back. As the fighters were bringing him

that they were going to try to break out the back of the camp and go over the mountains to safety. The people in the camp said, "Let the girls go with the fighters" – because they were frightened about what would happen to the girls if they were taken prisoner. I could not go because my wound was now blinding me in my right eye. The first group of fighters and girls went out at sunset but we were told that all had been captured and killed. But the second group had to try to go, and they left at night. I have not seen any of them again, either.

'At six in the morning we decided to surrender. There were no men left who could fight, and the first group of old men and women and children went out in the direction of the cemetery. While we were waiting our turn to leave, a *shibel* of about nine years old came back. He said they had killed all the people who had gone to the cemetery. He had been at the back, and hid and watched. The Phalangists had chairs in the cemetery and they made the people sit on them, then they cut their throats with their knives.'

There is always a point in interviews with almost any Palestinian about his or her life when you feel like very often, because stories of personal tragedy are commonplace among Palestinians and they are not a people who pour out their woes to every passing stranger. When I pressed her to tell me what had happened to her, the story came out like the playback of a recording made on a new tape with fresh batteries, every tiny detail clear and fresh, events described in chronological order with the tiniest details about the colours of clothes, the shape of faces and the inflections of voices. I heard my first stories about life in Tal Zaatar literally within hours of the destruction of the camp; but this one put all the others into context; it had a completeness that made me think that if I were to use it, I would not need to go to someone fresh from the horrors of

closing your notebook. You want to stop because you think to yourself, I've heard it all before, I've written it all before, and it moved world opinion about as far as I moved the Great Pyramid of Cheops last time I leant against it. The reason Randa held me was that her story had a terrifying freshness and clarity about it, as if what she was describing had happened last week, not six years previously. I suspect that it was not a story she had told Chatila and ask him to re-live his experiences. By the end of 1982, Randa knew how to live with her memories of what had happened in Tal Zaatar, and she wanted other people to know about them; she especially wanted a foreigner to hear what she had to say, so she was prepared to spend four hours while we went through the tedious business of having questions and answers translated from English to Arabic and back. Clearly, she saw

91

'What can we do? We will have to kill ourselves' — Randa

it was important that she kept this story very carefully within her so that it could be passed on to the next generation. There was an intensity about her that reminded me of the concentration-camp survivors whose faces, when you see them repeating their stories on television, tell you that only the memories of what happened in the camps and their need to tell what happened are keeping them alive.

'We were still waiting to go. There was my mother, who was pregnant, my two-year-old brother and my two sisters, Georgette and Rose – for some reason my mother gave all us girls Christian names, although we were Muslims. My real name is Rosalind. We started to walk out, and the Phalangists came to meet us. There were bodies on the ground – but it was somehow normal to see bodies on the ground. These were bodies that had been there for several days, because we could see where the cats had been eating them. The cats were very fat in Tal Zaatar because they ate the bodies, and they were dangerous because they would attack people – they had got used to eating people. Even the cats had become our enemies and the fighters used to shoot them. We were all afraid of them because we thought their teeth would be poisoned by eating the bodies.

'The Phalangists gathered us all together in one big building – I think it used to be a school to train the staff of hotels. Then they took all the young boys and old men to one side and began to question them. One of them was my grandfather who was over sixty. He had never been a fighter but he had always kept a room open in his house for the fighters and the young men, and you would always find some of them there, drinking tea and coffee, and talking; everyone knew him. The women pleaded for him, but one of the Phalangists said, "Al Dhoukhi, come on," because they knew he came from a fighting family. When he stepped forward in front of us all, one of them took his bayonet and brought it down on the top of his head. The blade went through the top of his head and the point came out of the bottom of his chin. Then the man pulled the bayonet forward and it split my grandfather's face open. The blood poured out, but I think he was still alive; he walked about three steps and, as he did, they shot him in the back. He fell on the ground on his face and his *khaffiyeh* fell off as his head hit the ground. Then someone said that he was not sure if this was al Dhoukhi after all, so they took hold of another old man who was about my grandfather's age and pushed him away, and as he walked in front of them they all shot him with their machine-guns.'

For the first time in almost an hour, she stopped talking. Then she took a very deep breath, sighed very deeply, and went on. 'At 11.40 a.m., the Phalangists brought back the first group of fighters who had tried to get out over the mountain. My father was one of them; they had brought them from Dekwani. They kept them all together, and for about one hour there was a lot of confusion because the last little group of Palestinians was fighting from a building at the edge of the camp, and the Phalangists were running around, firing in all directions and running through the buildings we had left, looting what was left behind. At one o'clock some Tigers of the National Liberal Party arrived, led by an official (whose name she gave but who would probably sue if it was repeated here, and whom I would gladly name and fight in the courts if I thought for one moment it would change Lebanese history by a billionth of a millimetre, but it won't, so I won't) whose brother had been killed in the earlier fighting around the camp. They shot some of the men and dragged off some of the girls, but then some trucks from the Arab peacekeeping force arrived to take people to safety and they started to load people on them. My father was on one of the trucks and it was about to go, when one of the National Liberal people started shouting, "Come out, Ibrahim al Dhoukhi." My father started to get down from the truck and, as his foot touched the ground, they shot him, first in the back of the head and then in the back. I remember he was wearing his brown nylon jacket and how the blood spread over his back. My younger sister started to cry, "Father, oh, Father," and we told her to be quiet, because she had very short hair and we thought they would shoot her because she looked like a boy. Then they asked all the rest of the people to get down from the truck, and they all got down. While we were waiting with these people, they brought back another group of fighters, and in this group was my cousin, Hossam Mahmoud al Dhoukhi, who was nineteen, and my brother, Haithum, who was eighteen.

'My cousin was dressed all in black, and I saw him first and then my brother. All of them had their hands up. They were made to stand on a low wall and were left to stand there in the sun. After a while, my cousin who was very thirsty asked for a drink and a girl called Muna Mashour who loved him ran out to him with some water. They dragged her away, and nobody has ever seen her again. Then a Phalangist woman who was all in black also was brought to the fighters. She must have had a son or a husband who was killed in the fighting. She was screaming and crying and she took her shoes off and started hitting the fighters with the high heels. Then the Phalangist fighters started joining in, hitting our men with pistols and rifle-butts. There were nine of our men, and they were beaten until they fell off the wall. Then they tried to make them march away with them, and the first one was my cousin Hossam, but he was beaten so badly he could not walk. They kept hitting him and calling him very bad words. When he fell, my brother, Haithum, ran to help him. When Haithum ran to help, so did the rest of our fighters, and then the Phalangists opened fire on them. We all fell to the ground to escape the firing; and we all lay there, covering our heads. When we looked again, all the Palestinians were gone. We have never seen any of those people, Haithum, Hossam, Riad, for seven years; but after seven years we still have not lost hope. We have heard that Saad Haddad still has prisoners, and the Syrians and the Phalangists, so maybe they are still alive. They killed one more old man, by jamming a broken bottle down on his head, and I had to walk in my bare feet through his blood to get to the truck that was going to take us to west Beirut. Some trucks went, but the Phalangists stopped our truck and made some of us get down. My mother was one of them and she got down with Rose and my little brothers; I was left on our truck with Georgette. Our truck drove away and I heard my mother shouting, "God go with you," as we drove across the crossing at the museum. We all met again two months later, but just then we thought we had lost everything. I kept thinking, "What can we do, we will have to kill ourselves?"'

Randa stopped for a drink of water. I had to borrow some sheets of notepaper, because I had filled my note-book. I am transcribing these notes now, and when I realize how much I have written already, I wonder how much farther I should go on. Do people get tired of hearing stories like this, or should you put them down in every minute detail, so that some sort of record will remain? She wanted to finish it; I wanted to hear what happened . . . You can stop reading if you like . . . but I promise this will be the last massacre story; you won't get all the blood and gore repeated over again when I have to talk about the final massacres in Chatila and Sabra. One story is enough, repeating six others won't make any more impact.

Randa, fourteen years old, bare feet covered with dried blood, dragging her small sister by the hand, arrived with a crowd of hysterical refugees on the west Beirut side of the green line, the crossing-point near the national museum in the centre of the city. 'The Palestinian fighters were waiting for us, and they kissed us and hugged us and people started to come to look for their relatives and friends, and there was someone for everyone except us. We walked along the streets, then one woman called Um Khaled came to us and said to us, "What village in Palestine are you from?" and we said we were from near Safad and she said that she came from there as well. She took us to her house in Bourj Abu Haida and told us we could stay with her. Then she took us to the P.L.O. radio station and we spoke on the radio and asked anyone from the al Dhoukhi family to come and fetch us. Nobody came, but Yasser Arafat was told about us and he ordered Fateh to help us and Um Khaled. I'll never forget Um Khaled, she took me to hospital every day so that they could heal my head-wound, and she looked after us like a mother. And in two months' time, my mother heard about us on the radio and came to get us. She had gone to Baalbek and had not been able to hear very much news.'

So Randa had escaped and was safe at last . . . Well, not really. One of the more grotesque ironies of life for the people of Tal Zaatar was that they were almost all resettled in Damour, a town south of Beirut. This had once been Christian, but its people were expelled, and some massacred, by the Palestinians and Lebanese leftists as a reprisal for an earlier massacre by the Christians of Muslims in the Beirut suburb of Karantina. By the time Randa's mother and her children got there, Damour was a ghost town, houses blown up, the walls of those still standing blackened by smoke and pock-marked with bullets. 'We were moved into a place – you couldn't call it a house: it had no doors or windows and there was dried blood on the walls. The P.L.O. gave us blankets, and we all slept together on the floor for the first few nights until the P.L.O. put in windows and a door and gave us some beds. We got money from them because of the men in our family who had been fighters and who were killed. I started to work in the pharmacy of the Arab Liberation Front and the smaller children went to the school in Damour. I met my husband, Ibrahim, in the A.L.F., we were married in 1979, and I went to Beirut. But my mother stayed in Damour with my brothers and sisters until the Israelis bombed them out in June of this year. Once again, she left everything behind and took with her only the children – children have been the only possessions she has ever managed to keep; to us Palestinians, they are the only important possessions. I was living in Beirut then, but my mother could not come to me because I was living near the sports stadium near Chatila camp and the Israelis shelled and bombed it every day. So I left on 10 June. I took a few clothes because I thought I'd be back, but here I am in Baghdad and all I have from Beirut is these clothes. We Palestinians always seem to leave, thinking we will soon be back, and we never seem to go back. We were always told when we were children about how our parents and grandparents left Palestine in 1948: they always used to tell us how they left fruit on the trees and kettles boiling on the stoves and food in the ovens because they expected to be back in a few hours, and they have been away ever since. I have nothing to go back to in Beirut. After we left our apartment there in June, a bomb came through the roof and down three floors before it exploded, and blew the kitchen and the living-room apart.'

The Auschwitz and Treblinka stories are the ones that finally pushed the West into creating Israel; Randa's story is the kind that should one day help give the Palestinians somewhere to feel safe. At least a story like hers is an answer to that bloody silly question that writers of letters to papers and news-magazines love to ask: 'Why is it that the Arabs, with all that money and all that land, can't let the Palestinians settle in their countries and let Israel live in peace with its tiny share of the Middle East?' The answer, of course, comes from Randa and everyone else in Chatila or Tal Zaatar or Sabra who have spent their whole lives in an Arab country and have nothing but death and disaster to remind them of their stay. As Randa said, and most Palestinians do, 'Only in a country of my own could I feel

Reunion

safe. I have never felt safe in my life. I lived in Beirut, now I live in Baghdad; but these places are not my homes, they're my problems.'

Finally, I asked Randa whether she would let her son, whose name is Lou'ai and who is two and a half, join the P.L.O. as a fighter. Typical journalist's question . . . and she answered exactly as I knew she would, because I've heard it from maybe fifty Palestinian mothers, and the answer is the reason why the Palestinians will either get a state or literally be exterminated as a people: 'If we cannot get a Palestine state by any other way, it is not a question of whether I would let him fight. He will have to fight.'

Suddenly she stopped talking and, from sitting almost bolt upright in her chair, she sagged back and closed her eyes. Someone came in from an outer office with tea and a book published by the Arab Liberation Front to commemorate their own fighters who had been killed in Tal Zaatar. It must have had about 300 pictures in it, mostly family pictures, and every now and again a cut-out from an A.L.F. poster where no picture existed. We started to turn the pages: Adib al Dhoukhi, born 1952, killed in Tal Zaatar; Ahmed Mohammed al Dhoukhi, born 1943, killed in Tal Zaatar; Hossam Mahmoud al Dhoukhi, born 1958, killed in Dekwani; Haithum al Dhoukhi, born 1960, killed in Tal Zaatar – that last was a very poor photograph, so someone had drawn in details over the blurred image, which made her brother look very European, blond and soft-featured. Then Ibrahim Mohammed al Dhoukhi, born 1951, killed in Tal Zaatar – there had obviously never been a picture of her father, so the layout artist had substituted a section of a poster showing Begin and Sadat embracing; Mahmoud al Dhoukhi; Amar Ahmed al Dhoukhi; Suleiman Mohammed al Dhoukhi. As we turned the pages, Randa got up and stood behind us. The only time I saw her crack even slightly was when she ran her finger over the improbable picture of her brother. 'It's not a matter of whether you're born lucky or unlucky. It's whether you're born Palestinian.'

Mirvat Sharfiye in Bourj Barajneh

7
Niggertown

It was Baha, the bearded twenty-two-year-old who was always laughing, the one from Bourj Barajneh camp who had been fighting for half his life for a country he had never seen – 'Well, I saw Palestine once – on television' – who told me the joke that gives this book its title. There was a small group of us and we were telling national jokes: Australian, Lebanese, French, when Baha told us the Palestinian joke. God called Ronald Reagan, Leonid Brezhnev and Yasser Arafat before him and told them he would answer one question from each. Reagan went first; he wanted to know when an American would be made president of the whole world. God told him it would happen in fifty years – and Reagan cried. God asked why he was crying, so Reagan told him, 'Because it won't happen in my lifetime.' Then it was Brezhnev's turn; he asked when the world would be totally communist. God told him that it would happen in a hundred years. So Brezhnev cried, and when God asked why he said, 'Because it won't happen in my lifetime.' Then God turned to Yasser Arafat and asked to hear his question. Arafat said, 'I want to know when my people will have a homeland of their own.' And God cried.

That's a real ghetto joke. Change the date and location, and it could have been told in Soweto or Montgomery, Alabama, or in Warsaw in the 1930s. It is the sort of joke that can only come from people in the most awful trouble who refuse to admit defeat. A broken people couldn't tell a joke like that because it wouldn't be a joke, it would be an admission of defeat and the loss of hope. It's a 'things couldn't be worse, but we're still alive' joke. I heard it before the war ended, sitting around the pool at the Commodore very late one night, drinking warm beer and feeding the last bits of beef gristle to the cats that prowled out of the deep

shadows. I laughed then because it is funny, but I don't think I appreciated it fully until I went back to the camps after the massacres, on my way back from Baghdad, on the way back from yet another war.

We were standing in the narrow dirt road outside Abu Moussa's *falafel* stand in Sabra camp when we heard the roar of a high-powered car from around the next corner. Abu Moussa's son-in-law suddenly jumped out of our group, grabbed a little girl who was stumbling across the road and threw himself and the child into the opposite doorway. The car missed them by about two feet. It was a white Mercedes, flying red, white and green Lebanese flags from the twin rear aerials, and the whole back windscreen was plastered with photographs of the new president, Amin Gemayel. It went past us at close to 40 m.p.h.; the driver in his white suit and dark blue open-neck shirt didn't pause and didn't even turn his head as he drove past.

I see from my notes that this was 23 November 1982, a little over two months after the Israelis finally pushed into west Beirut and their Christian allies carried out the massacres in Sabra and Chatila. I was not there during the killings; but now I was back to talk to people about what had happened. We were with Abu Moussa simply because he was the first man we came across who wanted to talk about present conditions in the camps. After we had regrouped, he looked in the direction of the passing car and said to me, 'If he had hit that baby, he wouldn't have stopped. He was Lebanese, and there is a different law for us and them now. If he had killed that girl I don't think anyone here would have even gone to the police, because they know they wouldn't have got any help.'

My friend Godfrey Hodgson, who was a great traveller in the southern states of America, once told me how he was taken on a tour of the 'nigger-town' of Montgomery,

Chatila, winter 1982

Alabama, by a white crony of George Wallace's. He was a lawyer who wanted to show Godfrey how happy the blacks were to have good old George in charge; they roared through the shanties late at night, with people diving off the roads to avoid being run over. Eventually they stopped outside one darkened hut; the lawyer got out of his car, went up to the front door and pounded on it until a frightened black man came cautiously to the door. 'Hey, boy, I'm with Governor Wallace, and I want you to tell my friend Mr Hodgson here how happy you folks are to have Mr Wallace as Governor' was how the conversation began, and it was followed by a stumbling five-minute speech from the shaking black man about how happy indeed he was to go to bed each night, knowing that the Governor was up there at the state house looking after his interests.

The Palestinian camps have now become Beirut's nigger-town. People cower out of the way when cars flying Lebanese flags use the narrow dirt roads as a speedway; the police raid the area almost daily; in the winter, when I was there, by four in the afternoon the whole area suddenly emptied of men and boys between fifteen and fifty because the favourite police tactic for making arrests was to grab people after dark and in winter, darkness fell early. As darkness comes the men filter out and move towards the centre of Beirut, where they stay with friends, or even sleep out in doorways and in the open, rather than wait at home for the midnight knock on the door.

It wasn't so long ago that the camps were almost independent city states, places where reporters like myself couldn't go unless we had P.L.O. permission – and often a P.L.O. guide as well. The Israelis are quite right when they say that the Palestinians created a state within a state; they did, of course, in the camps and in large chunks of south Lebanon. The real point is that every major segment of Lebanese society created a state within a state for themselves as the real state broke up. The Maronites under Bashir Gemayel had a state north of Beirut with its own taxes and militia; Major Haddad, the Lebanese puppet of the Israelis, had his own little kingdom in the south; Suleiman Franjieh, the former president, controlled a fiefdom around his mountain fortress of Zghorta in the north; and Walid Jumblatt had inherited the Druse kingdom up in the mountains southeast of Beirut when his father was assassinated. Each of these little kingdoms grew stronger as the central state collapsed; in the end, if you were a journalist you carried half a dozen passports: bits of paper or cardboard printed with the emblems of the various militia and permissions to enter. The wise journalist kept the Christian passes from Gemayel's Phalangists and Chamoun's Tigers and Akl's Guardians of the Cedars in his right-hand pocket and the passes from the P.L.O. and the P.F.L.P. and the Jumblattis in his left. Nobody got shot for showing a P.F.L.P. pass to a Phalangist, but it certainly screwed up easy access when you got your papers wrong.

During the war, we went to the camps almost every day: they were the major targets of the Israeli attacks, and they were either on the front line or pretty close to it – in some places the front lines were no more than twenty to thirty yards apart. The last Israeli prisoner to be taken by the Palestinians during the war had been captured right on the edge of Bourj Barajneh. I talked to a Palestinian intelligence officer later who told me that Private Ronnie Aoush had just wandered straight into their positions. The kids who captured him thought he was stoned out of his mind on hash, something the Israelis had started to get a real taste for. Maybe but, high or straight, he had only to walk a few yards in the wrong direction and he was in trouble.

The camps are the Palestinian homeland until the real one comes along. They're camps in the sense that the people who live in them believe they are camping out until they go home; they're not regarded as permanent. They are tent cities no longer, but closely packed suburbs of cement-brick houses with narrow, winding, dirt streets, rarely more than about ten feet across. They're badly drained and the gutters stink; in winter the dirt roads become bogs, most of the houses have power only when the owners can make an illegal connection to the power mains, and many of them today don't have running water: during the day the narrow alleys are always crowded with women and girls carrying plastic containers for water on their heads.

They are, naturally, festering hell-holes, totally contaminated with the evil virus of Palestinian nationalism. It is here that Palestinian kids hear from their old grannies the stories of how they were driven off their land by the Jews in 1948. The young children absorb these stories about the loss of their birthright from the time they begin to understand what is being said; by the time they are ten, like Farouk, most of them are starting some sort of military training. Every year or so we would do a piece in the magazine about where the Palestinians were going, and I would go down to the camps and tour the area, and I'd talk to the old people about their property in Palestine and to the twenty-five-year-olds about the latest round of fighting up in the mountains; they'd offer me thyme-flavoured tea, and very likely a blushing twelve-year-old girl in a headscarf and brilliantly coloured floor-length skirt and blouse would come in with her A.K.-47 and demonstrate to me how she could dismantle the thing and put it together again in two minutes while the rest of the family watched intently, waiting to burst into applause when the last component was snapped into place. After that, it was quite likely that the youngest son, who had never been outside Beirut in his life, would tell you he was a Palestinian from Haifa, and he would tell you his grandfather's story about the exodus as though it had happened to himself just the week before.

It probably has a lot to do with the quality of the

Ibrahim

Fadhi Salim

translation that these stories either came out very flat or in such bursts of over-heated rhetoric that I couldn't believe they hadn't been carefully rehearsed, no matter who told them. But when you see the old people telling their woes in Arabic, you see them become angry then tearful then resigned; and you get the message, as their grandchildren so clearly do, even if you can understand only one word in six.

In Bourj Barajneh in August at the height of the bombing, I recall meeting a wild-eyed old man called Maha al Haj Ibrahim. It was an odd meeting: we were walking down the main shopping street at the edge of a camp when we were surrounded by a group of angry teenagers all carrying A.K.-47s and wanting to know what we were doing in the area. One of them shouted at us that, every time a photographer came into the district, the visit was followed within hours by an Israeli air-strike. We were fumbling for our P.L.O. passes when Maha al Haj Ibrahim came out, grabbed me by the arm, shooed the kids away and invited us into his house down a small side-street.

He took us into a high-ceilinged, pale blue room, a couch down one side, a garish nylon hanging with the image of the Dome of the Rock on one wall, a low sideboard with a tray of gold-rimmed tea-glasses on it and a black-and-white photograph of a grey-bearded old man in a European suit with high collar and tie, and a white Arab head-dress. Maha al Haj disappeared into another room, probably his bedroom, then suddenly reappeared brandishing an A.K.-47 over his head in his left hand and carrying a red booklet in his right which he then handed to me. The booklet was a red-covered passport, printed in black on the cover, which had been his father's. On the front it read 'British Passport Palestine No. 130906'; and inside was an introductory note which read: 'Palestinian under Article One of the Palestinian Citizenship Order 1925'. The passport had been issued to his father, Mohammed al Haj, on 27 May 1940. It was, as he said dramatically, evidence that there had once been a Palestine; his only wish was that he too would have a Palestinian passport, like his father's, before he died.

Men like Maha al Haj Ibrahim are the keepers of the flame of Palestinian nationalism, even more than the Arafats and the Habashes who come and go as the Palestinian drama develops. There he was, waving his gun in the air, white-stubbled jaw out thrust, telling us the story he had told a hundred times to his four children and their friends in the neighourhood: how his father had smuggled him out of Haifa in 1938 when there had been a clash between Arabs and Jews, and how he had lived in Egypt until 1948 when he heard of the efforts to create a Jewish state and had gone back to fight with the Palestinians grouped near Haifa. 'We were north of Haifa, and it was just like it is today. There was shelling from the sea and land, and they dropped leaflets telling us to leave because our lives were in danger.' He shook

the A.K.-47 in real rage. 'If I'd had a gun like this in 1948, those Jews would never have kicked me out.' He lowered the gun and sat down and drank his coffee. 'I wonder how soon it will be before I have to fight here. Well, let the Israelis come and I'll see what I can do. Maybe next time we meet, we'll be able to go to Haifa

together and I'll walk down to Tel Aviv with you.'

He was a wild old man; his gestures and volubility brought back to me images of vaguely remembered Irish uncles when I was very young in Australia. He was certainly the sort who would have fought if he had to and with any luck he might have survived the bombing of Bourj Barajneh, although he was also the kind of stubborn old coot who would have refused to leave his house even when artillery was flying in every direction. I looked for him after the war, but the little streets look very much alike; the local people all said they didn't know him – I suspect that like all ghetto-dwellers, they

'I was in the kitchen when the plane came...my mother yelled...
I laid down on the floor covered with dust...I passed out...'
— Fadhi Salim

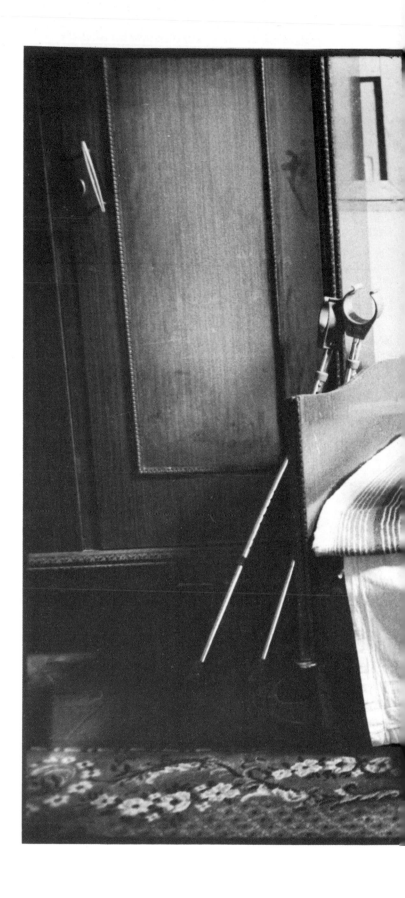

The peacekeeper — French soldier, Sabra 1982

'We were in a shelter, we thought we were safe' — Mirvat Sharfiye

Fatmeh Dakik — aged five

saw no reason to give their friend's name to a foreign stranger. I was to have the same trouble later in Chatila when looking for my warlike friend, Farouk. We drove within a few yards of his house and asked for him by name, but (as he told us later) nobody would have admitted knowing him because, under the new order, when people come looking for you they're not coming to do you any favours.

The camps are very nervous places today. The streets are too narrow for cars so you have to walk; the feeling you pick up immediately is not so much one of defeat as of suspicion and total lack of confidence. Young men who two months earlier would have challenged you if you took a side-turning now refuse to meet your gaze, or maybe they mutter an insult about 'Americans' under their breath as they walk past you. The very history of the war is now being washed away by the winter rains stripping walls which in August were covered with political posters, spray-painted with slogans and plastered with pictures of 'martyrs' of the revolution, the young and middle-aged men killed defending the camps. I started to write some names down before they disappeared; many were almost illegible already, the printing

washed out by rain and sun. There was always a photograph, usually a stiff, unsmiling face staring straight ahead as for a passport picture, and underneath the name of the man and his organization. 'Jamil al Haj, born 1954 in Aranta. Went to many military academy courses. Killed 13 February 1982 dismantling an explosive charge.' 'Martyr Ali Mohammed Said, born 1957 Bourj Barajneh Camp, killed 6 September 1980.' 'Comrade martyr Hussein Ali Kais, born Baalbek 1957, killed 29 December 1981.' 'Imad Afif Snounou, born 1956 in Bourj Barajneh, killed April 1982.' The last picture was of a boy of about ten . . . probably the only one the family had.

Occasionally I would be brought up short by the sight of the face of someone I knew. Peeling off the walls of the hospital for the mentally retarded in Sabra was a series of pictures of Abu Hassan who had been head of Arafat's personal security until the Israelis got him with a car-bomb as he very carelessly followed his usual route home to his Lebanese beauty-queen wife. Abu Hassan was a tall, gaunt, pale-faced young man who was almost always among Arafat's retinue when I went to see him. I remember him particularly because we once printed an

116

Ibrahim Koujok — aged twelve

Mohamed Kamel Snounou — aged thirteen

incorrect Mossad leak that Israeli agents had shot and crippled him for life. An exquisite young man in a blue velvet suit wearing a diamond-studded Patek Philippe gold watch came up to me in the lobby of the Commodore and murmured that Abu Hassan was very upset about the reports, and would there be any point in him writing a letter to the editor, saying that he was in fact in very good health?

In the next street, another face: Majid abu Sharer. 'Born Hebron 1936. Married and father of three children. Israeli criminal hands assassinated him on 9 October 1981 in Rome.' Majid was a high-level information officer for the P.L.O.; and I would occasionally interview him, although I always found him to be uncomfortable with foreign reporters: he tended to go on about 'the unyielding struggle of the valiant Palestinian people' when you asked him whether it was true or not that the Israelis had bombed Damour the day before.

I was slowly writing down the inscription on Majid's poster when an old woman grabbed my arm and shouted at me in Arabic. I asked what she was saying. 'She is asking you why you are bothering writing about the dead. She wants to know if you care nothing for the living.'

I suppose the extraordinary thing is that there are so many people still living in the camps. During the war we would watch as the Israeli jets bombed the camps throughout the day and then, late in the afternoon when the light had become too bad for the planes or in the very early morning before the pilots woke up, we would go down and pick our way through the fresh wreckage. Each day the route would be different, as whole streets would be blocked by falling buildings, yet always when we reached Sabra or Bourj Barajneh there would be people picking their way through the wreckage, salvaging a kettle here, a coffee pot there, a blanket or a tethered goat. Every day you would see people scrabbling in the still-smoking ruins and crushed bodies being dragged out of the rubble; but very large numbers of people lived throughout the war in the camps, and they refused to leave, even though the land and sea batteries poured thousands of rounds into the camps every day.

I once stopped to talk to a little man running a cigarette- and coffee-stand in a ruined street in Bourj Barajneh at the height of the war. He said he had been a tobacco planter near Acre and had walked north to Beirut after the Palestinians were driven out of northern Israel in 1948. I asked him why he stayed in such a dangerous area and he said, 'We civilians must stay to support our fighters. They must not be allowed to feel we have abandoned them.' I asked him his name and he said he could not tell me because he had a son who was an engineer in America, and he was frightened what Mossad would do to the son if they heard his father was living in the camp. 'Just write that my father's name was Al Qods [Jerusalem] and my mother's name was Palestine.'

Palestinians talk like that. It was on that same day that we were walking down an alley near the ruined Camille Chamoun sports stadium in Sabra when I saw a quite exceptionally beautiful girl; she told me her name was Leila Murad. She was wearing a violet blouse and a long skirt wrapped round her like a sarong; if I had seen her pale face and almond-shaped eyes in Asia, I would have said she was Burmese. She was coming out of the ruins of a small house, carrying a baby in one arm and a roll of blankets under the other, and she had a small child following her. She turned to me. 'Why are you photographing me, there is no tragedy in losing a house, as long as we have our guns we are not poor,' and she bent down and picked up a long flame-shaped piece of shrapnel, probably from a 155-mm. shell. She slashed through the air like a sword. 'If Ronald Reagan was here now, I'd cut off his head with this.' I asked her how old she was and if the children were hers. 'I am nineteen and the children are mine. I married young so that I could have many children to fight in the revolution.'

New York editors tend to see quotes like that and say, 'Oh, come on, what did she really say?' but simple people speak simply and don't bullshit around. I have no doubt at all that if Leila Murad survives until the end of the war she will have a dozen kids and some of them will join the P.L.O. and end up looking out from martyrs' wall-posters in some Palestinian camp or other. When you walk through the camps now, the first thing that strikes you is that there is a vast number of children everywhere: some playing, some carrying water, many of them helping rebuild ruined houses by carrying bricks or helping to level sites with rakes and spades. In a sense, the gunman who shot a five-year-old boy during the massacre and told his mother that he would only grow up to be a terrorist was right – if you define a terrorist as a man who fights for his country. Many of those kids will grow up with the memories of the bombing and mass-acres of 1982 to goad them into fighting, just as their parents are inspired, if that is the word, by the expulsion from Palestine in 1948 and massacres like Deir Yassin.

I was not in Beirut when the massacres happened; but when I heard about them, I wasn't surprised in any way at all – in fact, once the Israelis were allowed to break into west Beirut, the killings followed as naturally as they had in Russia during the Second World War when the Germans would burst into a village, and their Ukrainian or Hungarian *Einsatzgruppen* would follow them in to relieve them of the chore of killing off the women and children. I knew the massacres would happen, and I actually wrote that there would be killings in a note to my office in New York. I have a copy of the telex; it is dated 16 August 1982, a month before the massacres, and it discusses what the Israelis' plans for west Beirut might be. I thought then that the Israelis 'might wait until the Palestinians have come out of their positions and then launch the Phalangist Christian forces on the Palestinians when they are in the open. The Israelis would then say they had stuck to their side of the agreement but had no control over the forces of the host country, Lebanon . . . [This scenario] may seem improbable to you, but when you have seen just how murderous the Israelis are at first hand, you learn to distrust them very deeply indeed.'

There is not much point my writing a lot about the Sabra and Chatila massacres: I wasn't there, and this is supposed to be a book based on our own experiences. But even two months after it happened, there were plenty of signs that something awful had happened – I never knew blood had so much staying power until abu Moussa pointed to the wall across the road from his *falafel* stand. It was soft cement-brick and was pock-marked with bullets; he said that thirteen people had been lined up against it and shot. By a weird irony, someone had spray-painted a heart with an arrow through it and the initials 'K.C.' in English in the centre. From the bottom of the letters there was a great spray of dried brown blood that had sunk deeply into the porous surface, and two months later the heart still bled in the pouring rain of that day.

Sabra and Chatila will become part of the Palestinian group-consciousness, as have Deir Yassin and Tal Zaatar. The kids who walk past the bullet-pocked walls in the camps will be reminded that this was the place where their father died, here was where their cousin was shot, and this was where the Israelis stood while they allowed Haddad's men to kill their grandmother. In the camps, no matter who I spoke to, it was always 'Haddad's men', never 'the Phalangists' or 'the Kataeb', the Christian militia of east Beirut – although it is clear now that the Phalangists were the main killers, helped by a few of Haddad's men. Haddad's name is enough to cause panic, even now. Just before I got back to Beirut, someone who saw two strange cars turning into the abu Moussas' street suddenly started to shout that Haddad's men were coming back. There was total panic, with young men scrambling out of second-storey windows and desperately trying to climb high walls; screaming women started to drag crying children out of the houses and old people threw themselves in the street and began crying for mercy. For nights afterwards, people would take their bedding and carry it up to the positions held by the French and Italian soldiers of the multinational peacekeeping force now policing Beirut, because they thought they at least could keep them safe from the Christians.

In a sense, it is not all that important whether the killers were Phalangists or hit-men from Haddad. They were simply the butchers who killed the sheep after they had been led to them. It wouldn't have happened if the Israelis hadn't broken into west Beirut after the Palestinian fighters had gone; for them to say now that they didn't think the Christian militiamen would kill Palestinians if they got the chance is simply not credible. It seems fair to me that the Israelis have been widely condemned for allowing the massacre to happen, just as you blame the owner, not the alsatian, when it kills your cat. The importance of the massacre in historical terms is not that it showed up the Christians who did it as merci-less killers, but that it showed the Israelis to be utterly cynical about causing the deaths of hundreds of civilians. After Sabra and Chatila, the rest of the world found it much easier to believe the earlier reports that through-out the war the Israelis had conducted a merciless terror-campaign against civilian targets. A country that stands by while its proxies shoot five-year-olds would have no ethical problems at all in firing phosphorus shells into hospitals.

The camps presented a series of eerie contrasts when I was there in November, and my first day was the strangest: I had walked to near the edge of Chatila and come across a family having a picnic outside their house. There must have been fifteen people, men, women and children. In the centre was a tiny girl of about two, just able to walk and staggering from knee to knee, dressed in a brilliant scarlet dress with gold embroidery. There was a middle-aged man, probably the girl's father, pulling a roasted chicken apart, a group of teenage children, a middle-aged woman, and an old grandmother all in black and with blue tribal tattoos on her forehead and lower lip. The party was spread out next to what I assumed was a garden which had just been spaded for a winter crop like potatoes; the earth was freshly turned, soft, bright red. Then I saw a tattered Palestinian flag stuck in the middle of the patch which must have been fifty yards long by about thirty wide. I walked across to it, my feet sinking in the soft red earth. The flag stuck out of an almost disintegrated wreath and on it were two ribbons, each bearing a faded Arabic slogan. One read: 'The massacres of Sabra and Chatila, Mr Sharon, will make us all the more determined' and the other: 'We promise our martyrs we will continue the fight until

they were among friends and on familiar ground. That was another strange juxtaposition: you would see people carefully rebuilding houses, filling in shell-holes, putting back roofs just a few yards away from walls that still bore the bullet-holes from the time their friends and families had been stood against them and shot. On another walk, I was in Bourj Barajneh when three buff-coloured Land-Rovers blocked off a section of a narrow street and some fifteen Lebanese police piled out, kicked in the door of a house, and reappeared five minutes later with a young man of about eighteen, naked except for blue shorts, his hands tied together and a blindfold around his head. I asked a girl in the little crowd that had gathered who the boy was and what he had done. She didn't know – or wasn't going to tell me.

victory and the establishment of an independent Palestinian state under the P.L.O.'

I was standing on top of a mass grave of about 200 people who had been murdered in the massacre; it would be easy enough to believe that the picnicking family had probably known some of the people buried under that red earth. But as Farouk said later, where else were people to go? They didn't feel safe anywhere any more, but at least when they stayed in the camps

When I left Beirut in November, the first priority for everyone in the camps was to survive the winter. The main roads had been turned into rivers of grey shit because the bombing had wrecked what drains and sewers there were; the rain was pouring through broken roofs; the police were making regular runs through the streets, cutting the illegal wiring that is the only source of electricity for most people. Nobody had any money and there hadn't ever been much work since the civil war began, but at least before the siege, the P.L.O. paid its men. Now the P.L.O. has gone and men like abu Moussa make a few pounds a day selling *falafel* or hawking cigarettes on Hamra. People couldn't exist without food supplies from the United Nations refugee agency, but the people in the camps complain they only get about half what is sent to them – the rest is taken by Lebanese middlemen. More than anything, people feel helpless; their position today is as it would be for a black in America if all the civil rights legislation of the last thirty years had been repealed. Baha used to tell me how, when he was a little kid, the police used to walk through the camps ordering people to give them food, drinks, shouting at old men to bring their identification papers, slapping teenagers around if they didn't obey orders fast enough, arresting men without charges and then demanding bribes to release them. He told how the Palestinians at last began to feel secure when the P.L.O. armed them in the late '60s, and he predicted that if the P.L.O. pulled out, the camps would be back to being ghettos as they had been before the guns came. They are clearly like that now, made more miserable by the fact that they are half in ruins and nobody has any money – or confidence, for that matter – to make all but the most basic repairs. They know they have to live there because there is nowhere else to go, but nobody sees any sense in spending a lot of money rebuilding houses that might be knocked down under re-zoning laws, something that has already happened in Chatila. To be a poor man and have a Palestinian accent in Beirut today is to be like a black man in South Africa in 1982 or a black man in the deep south of the U.S.A. in 1935: the minute you open your mouth to talk to an official about some injustice is the minute most of them cease to listen.

Yet the people in the camps in Beirut, no matter how miserably they live, are infinitely better off than those Palestinians trapped in the camps and the cities further south, in that part of Lebanon now controlled by the Israelis and their puppet, Saad Haddad. The lynchings have already begun around Sidon as the campaign begins to drive middle-class Palestinians out of their homes in Sidon and the villages around it, back into the camps. By the end of February 1983, at least fifteen Palestinians had been killed: some hacked to death, some shot after being mutilated, two or three soaked in petrol and burnt alive. Posters signed by the ultra right-wing Lebanese group that calls itself the 'Revolutionaries of the Cedars' have recently been plastered all round Sidon, especially on the doors of Palestinian-owned houses. There is an uncomfortable fascist ring to the language used on these stickers: 'Noble sons of Sidon and its environs: Help us drive the strangers from the land of Lebanon, especially from your heroic city – the city of Sidon which was oppressed by Palestinian tyranny and sabotage. We shall accomplish our slogan, "No Palestinians in the land of Lebanon" .' Another poster is much more to the point: 'Every worthy Lebanese should

kill at least one Palestinian.'

This is in an area completely controlled by Israeli soldiers; I have seen their checkpoints everywhere, and it is obvious that Haddad's men are little more than water-boys. Yet it is clear a climate of hatred for the Palestinians is being allowed to build up – and the Israelis are doing nothing to stop it, although the United Nations have made official protests about what is going on. Middle-class Palestinians are being driven out of their homes by gangs of armed Lebanese, who tell them their property has been confiscated, and forced back into the ruined camps outside the city. When this campaign of expulsion first began, one or two people protested – and within days, they had been kidnapped and murdered. The now terrified remainder are fleeing back to the camps; but already they have become unsafe and the small Mia Mia camp has been badly damaged by huge explosions. I saw Tal Zaatar being slowly surrounded and finally destroyed, and I see all the signs appearing that we shall soon see another Tal Zaatar or Chatila.

If I were a Palestinian, I would have to be a Buddhist as well. I would not be able to put up with all that misery unless I thought the wheel was turning and that in the next incarnation I would be better off because I had suffered so much in this life. The Palestinians are frequently compared with the Jews, and there are many parallels in their existences. The Palestinians now, like the Jews once, are a people without a country, a people who have had to educate themselves better than anyone else to survive, who have clung together in their camps to keep the flame of nationalism alive, who have refused to integrate and to intermarry, who carry the hope of 'next year in Jerusalem' with them. I think one of the reasons why Begin in his madness launched the Israeli assaults on the Palestinians was because he could understand how dangerous a persecuted but united people like the Palestinians can be. If you were a European Jew, you would know how a people can keep an ideal alive; you would also know that, as long as a single Palestinian lived, the hope of a homeland would also live. Unless he was blind and deaf to newspapers and television and the intelligence reports of his own brilliant secret service, he must have known that it would be the children who would suffer first from dehydration when he ordered the water supply to Beirut turned off; he must have known it would be the children to starve first when he blocked the food going in; he must have known that civilian casualties would exceed military ones by ten to one when the bombs started raining down on Sabra and Chatila; he must have known that the Christian militiamen had murdered Palestinians in Tal Zaatar and were still nurturing their blood-feuds.

The major Israeli justification for the terror bombing of the camps and – if it comes to that – of west Beirut, was that the Palestinians had military installations in civilian areas and the Israelis could not be blamed if

Sohail — a schoolboy

civilian buildings were hit accidentally, because in reality they were aiming only at guns and tanks hidden among those buildings. Well, yes; Begin and Sharon were quite right, there were guns and tanks and fighters in civilian areas; it would have been impossible for them not to be there because the perimeter was so small that the two groups had to mix together. I can imagine what Begin's reaction would have been, had the German commander in Warsaw who directed the assault on the ghetto defended himself by saying he was shelling the area, not to kill civilians, but because there was a dangerous group of armed trouble-makers hiding among the civilian population. The Palestinians fell back on Beirut because it was their last refuge and because they wanted to defend their civilian population. The combined Palestinian and Lebanese battle in Beirut was a purely defensive action, fought by a people who knew perfectly well that if they caved in, their enemies would come in and slaughter them. The Palestinians didn't trust the Israelis or their Christian allies – and neither did the Lebanese left in Beirut, for that matter. I remember going to see Saeb Salam, who is no special friend of the Palestinians, on the evening of 12 August, a day when Beirut had been shelled and bombed from morning to night. He told us that the Palestinians wanted the French, Italian and American multinational peace-keepers to take up positions along the ceasefire lines five days before they started to evacuate so that they knew they would get protection from an Israeli sneak attack when they were in the open. 'The Palestinians want five days!' Salam said. 'We Lebanese want five days because otherwise the Israelis will come in and massacre us all. They want to finish off Beirut as the capital of Lebanon.'

There are still almost half a million Palestinians in Lebanon, half of them at least living in and around Beirut, all of them scarred by what happened in 1982. I am sitting 2,500 miles away in middle-class English comfort; but, even picking up a sweat-stained notebook or one of Catherine's pictures, I can be back in Beirut and hear the planes overhead. But if I still have to open my notebooks or shuffle through the pictures, any child still in the camps only has to look out of his window or walk to school to have it beaten into him what happened in 1982. The bloodstains are still on the walls; there are the bullet-holes and the shrapnel slashes. There is beautiful Fatmeh Jaber with her sleeve hanging limply over the stump of her right arm; there is Fadhi Salim standing on the edge of the crowd watching the kids play football, his right leg missing, unable to join in. You walk home and there is Mirvat Sharfiye picking her way precariously down through the rubble-strewn, steeply sloping paths of Bourj Barajneh, trying to adjust to crutches and that missing leg. Wherever you look, you see the living reminders of what the Israelis did to the camps and to the Lebanese Muslim suburbs around them that were turned into free-fire zones because the people who lived in them were so wilfully stupid as to refuse to get out of the way. Maybe it will be possible to comfort Fatmeh Dakik when she's a little older – she's five now and wouldn't understand why the cluster-bomb blew off her left leg and her left hand and killed her baby brother; maybe she will feel better if someone reads to her what the kindly old Ariel Sharon told the inquiry in Jerusalem: 'We tried as much as possible to strike at selective targets; if there were injuries to civilians, they were accidental and unintentional.'

Sorry about that, Fatmeh, and Mirvat, and Fadhi, and that other Fatmeh, and all those others who couldn't run fast enough, if you weren't terrorists – and of course we can't be sure because we know they get you young – then we didn't mean it. No, really . . . 'we exercised cautionary steps at all levels in order to guard against harming civilians'. Now that makes you feel much better, doesn't it?

When I look around the camps today, I think of Farouk telling me how he went to Baghdad at the age of eight to start his guerrilla training, and I think of Leila Murad telling me how she got married very young so she could have lots of children who would fight in the revolution. The bombing of the camps and the crippling of the children in them doesn't frighten those kids – it just provides another and fresher set of reminders of who the enemy is and what he will do to you. The fire that swept Sabra and Chatila and Bourj Barajneh and the camps of the south was like a forest fire that clears away the brush to make way for the new growth. The new crop will be the bitterest yet.

8
The Undefeated

One of the first things you learn as a reporter is that other people think you are leading a fascinating life. Your host says: 'This is Tony, and he's a reporter,' and the almost Pavlovian response comes back: 'You must meet all sorts of interesting people and go to all sorts of interesting places.' If you're feeling good and talkative, you agree that, yes, it is really fascinating, and you drop in a couple of lines about what Indira Gandhi said last time you met her, and how Saigon had changed when you went back there last year. And if you're weary and you've answered the question fifty times that week, you say, no, journalism has been screwed by lack of money and the telephone, and you don't meet anyone or go anywhere, but just spend nine to five in the office like any other wage-slave, rewriting the copy from the wire services.

Both responses are accurate. I've met great men and been present at great events; and I've spent days on telephones on stupid stories about what the rate of the pound against the dollar should be, and what is the real colour of Prince William's hair. If some time and motion study expert did a breakdown on how I'd used every working hour in the twenty-seven years since I first joined the *Benalla Standard* in north-eastern Victoria (published twice weekly; circulation in 1956: 3,000), he would find I had spent more of that time waiting about than actually working: waiting for planes, waiting for trains, waiting for presidents, waiting for generals, waiting for prisoners of war to be exhibited, waiting for the phone to ring, waiting for room service in some fleabag hotel in Damascus. For every hour of excitement and success there are ten of tedium and enforced idleness. There is no natural flow to life as a correspondent, rather you live a life of unconnected episodes. I think that this is a reason why journalists write such dull memoirs: there's no continuity, just a string of anecdotes going nowhere: '. . . I remember the day I met de Gaulle, he was wearing his two-star general's uniform and talking to Malraux. He nodded to me and I turned, and there was Chou En-lai, a small man, neat, precise, in an immaculate grey Mao suit — obviously made in Savile Row. It was the time of the Versailles summit, and as I walked through the Hall of Mirrors I passed Richard Nixon, a complex man who will be remembered as a great president. Seeing him reminded me of a story Harry Truman once told me — we were at the United Nations, and he had just come from a meeting with Ben-Gurion, that grizzled old lion of the desert I had first seen in a dusty *kibbutz* in the Negev. "Arthur," the old man had said to me, "I've been a few places and seen a few things . . ." '

'Been a few places, seen a few things' is a code I use when getting drunk with old friends like Stewart Dalby of the *Financial Times* before we settle back and start lying to impressionable young beginners about the good old days in Pnom Penh and Quang Tri and Vientiane. About the girls in the Golden Hands II Massage Parlour in Saigon, and the opium at Chantal's in Pnom Penh and the lesbian bar opposite the Trocadero Hotel in Bangkok, where the most extraordinary acts used to be performed in front of groups of middle-aged Japanese men and women tourists. I find I slip into many of my stories now like a night-club comedian telling the one about the gorilla and his mother-in-law for the seven hundredth time. I also sometimes find myself in the middle of some amazing tale about myself, only to realize that it didn't happen to me at all but to someone like Tom Aspel, a cameraman who was always in terrible trouble in free-fire zones. The trouble is, you hear so many stories — and many of them so often — that they start to become part of your own memories; your experiences and those of others overlap like images on a double-exposed film. It happens with all reporters and probably all professional tale-tellers; after a few years, the stories come back to you retaining their form but with the characters changed. I now find I am hearing stories I have told about other people being repeated to me with myself as the hero or victim rather than the narrator.

But just as most events tend to blur and fuse over the years, a few remain totally clear and fresh because they were totally different from anything else I have encountered. A handful stand out for me, some historic and others which were never specially important. I have absolutely clear memories of the assassination of Bobby Kennedy, the fall of Dacca to the invading Indian army, the collapse of Biafra, the retreat at Hué of the South Vietnamese Third Division, and the departure in triumph of the Palestinian fighters and their allies from Beirut just a few months ago. The last is clear in my memory because it happened recently, but it has the same special quality as the others in that as I watched it happen I knew I was seeing something I would never forget.

There was an episode in each of the earlier events which fixes them with a special freshness in the mind. I was within a few feet of Bobby Kennedy when he finished his victory speech; and I followed him along with the usual team of press men and hangers-on, into the corridors leading to the kitchens of the Ambassador Hotel in Los Angeles. He was obscured by some hulking T.V. sound-man when suddenly there was shouting and the crash of breaking glass in front of me and, as always happens when there is a noise near a Kennedy, everyone started pushing and shouting and asking if he'd been shot. I turned to tell the man I didn't know and, as I did, my eye was caught by a television monitor. Although Kennedy was dying five feet from me, I saw him first on television, spread-eagled on the floor.

In Biafra I had made it to the edge of the Niger River across from Onitsha just after the surrender and the first starving survivors started to cross the river . . . You can read a thousand books about the fall of the Weimar Republic and the fact that you needed a billion German marks to buy a loaf of bread and a wheelbarrow full of new notes to buy a stamp, but it all stays unreal that way. It became real when a starving black man in a pale grey, dirty linen safari suit suddenly rushed up with a thick bundle of five-pound notes, the blue notes with the orange sun of Biafra, and pushed them at me, saying, 'I want food for my children, buy these souvenirs,' and I give him the equivalent of $1 for what last week was worth $5,000. In Vietnam, I was in Hué when the Vietnamese Third Division defending the northern approaches suddenly had a moment of collective panic in 1973. Just as a shoal of 10,000 individual small fish all turn simultaneously away from you in the same direction as you swim towards them, so the 6,000–7,000 men of

the Third Division all broke and ran at once down Highway One, a vast stream of men on foot, on bicycles, in commandeered cars and army vehicles of all kinds, A.P.C.s, two-and-a-half-ton trucks, jeeps, motorcycles. I have already forgotten why they ran at that time . . . whether there was a special offensive or not. What I will always remember is that when they had passed, as far as the eye could see, Route One to the north was like a piece of gold-shot green damascus silk, glittering in the sun. The road was carpeted with the green trousers and jackets thrown off by the retreating soldiers as they rushed to shed their military identity; the glitter was from the brass of tens of thousands of rifle, machine-gun and artillery shells dropped on the highway as they ran.

The fall of Dacca was important for me because it was the first time I had ever been caught in a besieged city: Dacca was different because, unlike what happened in west Beirut, the press corps who had decided to stay were trapped in the city with the bad guys – the Pakistanis who had been murdering and raping their East Pakistani subjects for the past year – while the good guys, the Indian regular army, was on the outside trying to get in. I started then to learn the lessons about where to go and where not to go during air attacks on built-up areas; started to learn something about gauging the morale of besieged soldiers; and heard for the first time that enormous thud of an exploding bomb in the middle of the night that has you bolt upright in bed, your eyes open before your dream has had time to evaporate. My obsession about head-shots began there: I was watching when a group of Pakistani prisoners, still carrying their guns because the Indians feared the outraged locals would lynch them all if they were defenceless, for some reason panicked and opened up on their captors. There was a thirty-second fire-fight; when it cleared, on one side there was a dead Sikh officer in a jeep, his turban blown off and his long hair falling over his face like a girl's, and on the other side of the road a dead Pakistani, shot through the head – the blood flowing and flowing and flowing from his utterly still body. And the other thing I remember was the sudden appearance of hundreds of women. I'd entirely forgotten about women in that city because I had been there so long without seeing any. But suddenly the city was free of their tormentors, and the women in their brilliant saris had all come out of their cellars and the inner rooms and corridors of their houses; and there they were in the streets, the fluttering saris glowing in the clear December light, waving and throwing flowers at the dusty Indian soldiers who were grinding in their tanks into the city to free them.

The whole of the Palestinian departure is so fresh in my mind that a single episode has not yet crystallized out in my memory, although eventually time will blur the less dramatic events and make others more important. It could be that in five years' time I will look back on those days and realize that the most important thing I saw was

the friendly handshake between the colonel commanding the newly landed American marines and the Palestine Liberation Army colonel in charge of the western sector of the Beirut port. Looking back after just five months, I can see the whole complex withdrawal only as a single event; seen like this, the most important thing about it was that it was the first time the world saw an undefeated Arab army marching away in triumph with their guns over their shoulders, after fighting a full-scale war with the Israelis. Until August 1982, Arab–Israeli wars had always ended with the Israelis holding the guns and watching the long lines of defeated Arabs, their hands in the air, straggling away to surrender.

That pull-out started very much later than it should have. The Palestinians had agreed to leave by the end of July, and the Lebanese negotiators dealing with them were happy with the terms of the withdrawal. The Israelis on the other hand, stalled for time continually, because they wanted to stop the Americans from thinking about the West Bank settlements, because they wanted to consolidate their grip on the south and because, like gamblers throwing their last few pounds into the poker pot, they thought their next push would be the one to finally crack the Palestinian defences. Saeb Salam used to keep us up to date on what was happening in the talks with the Lebanese, Americans, Israelis and the P.L.O.; each night he would come in, steaming with rage about some new Israeli ploy to keep the battle going. One day they would object to the French peace-keepers coming in before the Palestinians left – the French would allow the fighters to hide weapons and leave men in the city before they left, they claimed. They argued about the true strength of the Palestinian forces, saying they didn't believe they were all going to leave. One night, Saeb Beg stomped in at the point of apoplexy: the Israeli delegate wanted the name of every one of the 13,000 fighters who were supposed to be leaving, and he said Israel couldn't allow anyone to leave on 'D' (for departure) day. 'They actually say,' said Saeb, 'that "D" Day has connotations of victory because of the Second World War. So they say they can't think of a ceasefire until it's changed to something noncontroversial like "E" for exit day.'

The time they bought by their procrastination and nitpicking enabled the Israelis to launch their most savage attacks of the war. On the evening before 12 August, which was a day of mindless slaughter with wave after wave of air-raids and no attempt by the Israelis to move on the ground, we went up for our usual briefing from Saeb Beg. We sat in the cool in his little office (he had his own generator, so this was one of the few air-conditioned offices in the city) and asked him if he thought that an agreement on withdrawal had finally been reached. He said that in theory there was an agreement – in fact, there had been for some time, but he was still fearful. 'I for one have great fear of the Israelis not withdrawing, except with great difficulty. Even at the last moment I would not rule out Sharon, Shamir and Begin destroying Beirut – making it a *fait accompli*. They want the partition or disintegration of Lebanon, then they would have hegemony over us.' Perhaps he had a premonition of the horrors of the next day; he is, after all, over eighty and has lived through Turkish rule, French rule, and has been Prime Minister of Lebanon. He knows Beirut better than almost anyone in the city and he said suddenly, 'My heart bleeds for Beirut all the time. This was once a beautiful and prosperous town; now it is a city of ghosts.'

The following day there was that last great climax of Israeli violence; Reagan was goaded far too late into waving an admonitory finger in the direction of Begin, and the final ceasefire was called. The foreign peace-keeping troops were brought in to secure the port area, where the Palestinians were to embark, and to patrol the Damascus road to protect those going to Syria; the exodus began at last on 21 August.

The Palestinians left because there was no point in staying. Clearly, they could have held out for months – they had the food and ammunition needed to fight for that length of time; it was also obvious that the Israelis lacked the will to break into west Beirut. There is no doubt that had they concentrated their attacks in the southern sector, they would finally have battered through; but after that, they would have had to fight block by block, and they weren't prepared to die in the numbers needed to clear out heavily defended suburbs. What they undoubtedly would have done – and the firestorm of 12 August proved their intention – was to level west Beirut by air and long-range sea and land bombardment if the P.L.O. stayed. As Mahmoud Labady told me, the P.L.O. might have considered hanging on if they had thought they might be relieved by outside forces; but it was obvious that this was not going to happen. Abu Iyad said in a message on 31 July, 'The Palestinian Lebanese people are being exterminated every day through a medical and vital-supplies blockade, by the cutting of water and electricity, by uninterrupted military attacks, yet the world remains silent. Where are the Arabs?'

As Mahmoud said, 'We're not the only people in this city. If it were ours, we'd turn this into Stalingrad and they would have to destroy every single building before we gave it up. But Beirut is Lebanese, and if we stay here the Israelis will destroy it. We know now that the outside world is not going to intervene to help us, so we will leave as soon as we are allowed to leave with honour. We owe too much of a debt to the Lebanese who have fought beside us in this battle for us to stay and give the Israelis an excuse to finish the destruction of the city.'

By leaving as they did, undefeated and unbowed, the fighters achieved what should be a major objective for any guerrilla: they survived to fight another day. Nevertheless, I think most of them would have preferred to stay and fight, and the kids were particularly bitter because, unlike their commanders, they had never known defeat. They had held off the Israelis in 1978 and, although they had retreated in the early stages of the 1982 campaign, they had finally made a stand and the Israelis had been stopped dead in their tracks. Just before they finally moved out for the last time, I went round to Mustafa's post and asked the man there if they wanted to go. In the beginning nobody would answer, until finally Khalil said, 'The leadership has said we must go, and we have to obey their orders.'

The same night, I had a beer at the Commodore with Bassam abu Sharif; I asked him whether he thought a pull-out was an admission of defeat. I told him the kids out near the front thought that they should have fought to the finish. He had to turn fully in his chair in order to face me, because he had lost an eye and half a hand when an Israeli book-bomb blew up in his face. 'You know, that's a real Israeli reaction, that feeling you should fight to the end. But we don't have that Masada complex, and we don't ever tell our people they have to stay in their positions and die in them rather than give up. I've never been able to understand the Israeli belief that it's better to commit suicide than be captured. There are times when any fighter knows he will probably have to die, because he has to make a stand to allow other people to escape or re-form a line. But we have this motto, "*Al watan houwa al hayat*", which translates as "The homeland is life", and we tell our people that if they're going to fight for the homeland, they have to stay alive to do it. If one of our men was surrounded by five Israelis, we'd expect him to surrender and start thinking about how to escape; we wouldn't expect him to pull out his gun and get himself shot. We tell them that one day they may have to die, but they shouldn't just throw away their lives to make a gesture.'

I told Bassam I had once been at Masada, and it was a very curious experience. It struck me immediately that there was a lesson for Israel to be learned at Masada – and it has nothing to do with the spiel the tourist guide gives you about how it is more glorious to die a free man than live to bend the knee to your captors. Masada is a flat-topped, red rock massif overlooking the Dead Sea; King Herod had turned it into a combination of fortress and holiday home. The flat top has storerooms, a synagogue and barracks and other military buildings, and at one end is Herod's summer palace, a series of observation- and living-rooms dropping in steps down the end of the mountain. You can see out for miles across the desert and the blue sea, and you can imagine what it was like on a summer evening, lounging back on the balcony, being fanned by Nubian slaves, and with a goodly supply of sixteen-year-old girls waiting to satisfy your every whim. In the background, the guide goes droning on about the significance of Masada; suddenly you stop dreaming what it must have been like to be Herod and start listening to what this man is trying to say.

The story is not about what a great time Herod had, but about the defence of Masada against the Romans. The Romans had colonized virtually all of the country and the only Jews to hold out were a band of Zealots, a group of religious fanatics and fighters under a Begin-like figure called Eleazar. Like good guerrillas, the Zealots kept falling back in face of the regular army, but finally (like the Palestinians choosing to make their last stand in Beirut) they climbed to the top of Masada, sealed off the access paths and told the Romans that this was where they would make their last stand. Like the Israelis in Beirut, the Romans stayed and surrounded the place; and the battle for Masada began. It was a long-drawn-out affair: the Jewish defenders had huge supplies of food and weapons, and the sheer cliffs were unclimbable, so that a lesser people than the Romans might have said to hell with it and let the Zealots keep their little patch of ground. But the Romans weren't like that; they decided to build an earthen ramp up to the top of Masada. There were, however, no Philip Habibs in those days, so the siege came to its inevitable conclusion. One day the last few buckets of earth were tipped out and the Romans brought up a battering-ram and started to smash through the walls around the summit. On the top of Masada, the Jews realized they were about to be overrun so rather than surrender and be led off as slaves, they killed themselves and, when the Roman commander reached the summit, all he found was a pile of corpses. This final mass-suicide has become an essential part of Israeli folklore, and its lesson to them is that it is better to die than bend the knee to the conqueror. Masada has become a place of pilgrimage for a militaristic nation; ace regiments like the paratroopers have firelit initiation ceremonies for new recruits among the ruins. I have seen pictures of the young paratroopers in their uniforms, lit by the flickering fires – they bring back very disturbing memories of the firelit ceremonies the Nazis used to hold in places of pilgrimage like Nuremberg.

The real meaning of Masada for modern Israel struck me as soon as the guide finished the story of the final hours of the defenders of Masada. Looking down, you can still see below you the clear outlines of the ancient Roman barracks that ringed Masada and how thoroughly it was surrounded and cut off. When you go to the back of the massif (the side facing away from the Dead Sea), you can still see the raised ground that is all that remains of the ramp. The lesson to me – which I saw immediately – is that Masada is Israel today: seemingly strong and secure within its boundaries, but completely surrounded by the hostile Arab camps. The ramp that took so long to build is Arab unity; it is being built very slowly, not so much out of the bricks of Arab love for Arab as out of the mud of Arab bitterness for the years of humiliation and death that have been poured on them by Israel. Just as the Zealots once shook their fists at the tiny Romans below, so Menachem Begin struts and screams from his apparently inpregnable fortress on the Mediterranean. It took the Romans a long time to build the ramp but, once it was completed, they were able to make the final breakthrough. I think the same will happen with Israel, while it is run by men like Begin: they won't bend, and the Arabs will finally get their act of men, money and trust together . . . and that will be it. Like the Romans, the Arabs have all the time in the world and, again like the Romans at Masada, they have only one battle to win.

Yasser Arafat decided fairly quickly that Beirut was not going to be the P.L.O.'s Masada. He and his men hung on until it became clear their line would not be broken unless the Israelis were prepared to die in thousands rather than hundreds, then he decided to go for a deal that would allow him and his men to live to fight another day. Begin and Sharon, beside themselves as they watched the Palestinians preparing to slip away, tried everything to stall for time and to stop the Americans, the Lebanese and the Palestinians doing a deal; although they *were* able to buy time to kill a lot more civilians, they didn't get Yasser and his men. The Israelis' last desperate throw was to ask for the name of every one of the 13,000 fighters who were leaving, but even the Americans couldn't buy that and the great exodus finally began on 21 August.

The fighters started appearing on Hamra about a week before they finally left, as they realized they were shortly to be heading for a lot of funny places most of them had hardly heard of. Syria, okay; Iraq, fine; but North Yemen? Everyone was buying suitcases and portable radios and new jeans and bottles of booze – the street got completely clogged as the street-vendors were pushed on to the road by men and women carrying loaded suitcases in one hand and A.K.-47s in the other. A friend of mine who had been born in Chatila camp and had never been anywhere in the Arab world but Damascus was suddenly told he was going by ship to Hodeida in North Yemen. He was wondering whether to buy himself a record-player: 'I don't know if they have electricity in North Yemen. All I know is, they sit around all day chewing *qat* [a leaf with a mild stimulant] and a story my uncle told me about an old Imam who ran the country after the Second World War. He asked his advisers to tell him how he could get American aid: they told him that North Yemen would have to declare war on America; then, when the Americans won the war, they would rebuild the place like they did Germany. But, said the old man, what will happen if Allah wills it that we defeat the Americans? Where will we get the money to rebuild the United States?'

I knew some fighters who were glad to be going, others who were pissed off, and others who were scared. The ones who were glad to go just wanted to get out and back into the battle, into the Beka'a, across the border into Israel. The ones who were pissed off tended to fall into one of two camps. The less realistic thought they

were winning and wouldn't have to wait much longer before the Israelis decided to pack up and go. The cooler ones thought they should stay to let Begin make an even bigger monster of himself than he had been already. They all listened to the Arab service of the B.B.C., and they knew that every day, as the killing went on, Begin was taking Israel further beyond the pale. The men who were scared were scared not for themselves but for the people they were leaving behind; some of them thought the Israelis would break in, round up all the Palestinians and deport them. The majority of the pessimists were obsessed with the idea that somehow the Israelis would use the Christian militiamen as their hired guns and turn them loose on the civilians in the camps. Nobody who had lived in Beirut through the civil war had any doubt that, given the chance, the militia would wade in and not stop shooting until nothing moved in Sabra and Chatila and Bourj Barajneh. The fear of vengeance was so strong, you heard it from just about every other departing Palestinian. We all filed the story about these fears, but nobody outside Lebanon took much notice . . . the fact is, when it comes to the crunch (maybe I should say 'came', because minds may have changed now) nobody in America could believe that Israel ('they fight hard but fair') could just stand by while a pack of gunmen slaughtered men, old guys, little kids and women by the hundreds.

But before anyone could leave, we had to wait for the foreign peacekeeping forces to arrive. There was going to be a three-nation force to keep the two sides apart: French Foreign Legionnaires, American Marines, and Italians from what is always described as 'the crack Bersagliere Regiment', who are famous for running instead of marching on ceremonial occasions and for the fact they have cocks' feathers on their parade helmets. The Foreign Legion came in first and the Italians last, and both lived up to preconceptions: the French looked exceptionally tough and ruthless in skintight uniforms, bare muscly arms, scars, loaded down with lethal hardware; the Italians looked a little ridiculous, in all-white vehicles – 'Valentino made the jeeps,' someone said – and white helmets which were functional enough but also had dead chickens plastered on one side, so that the troops looked as if they were wearing some bizarre form of cloche hat.

The U.S. Marines didn't look all that terrific. Apart from the guys who guard the front doors of American Embassies, I hadn't seen a Marine since Vietnam; up round Quang Tri I remember them as being pretty much built on the lines of the French Foreign Legion: big, hard, bristle-headed; good guys to have on your side when the fire came out of the tree lines. The Americans who came ashore to secure the Beirut port were a curious-looking bunch. First, they seem to have abolished height qualifications in the Marines, so there were plenty of men shorter than I am – which means they were about five feet five. All right, as the Vietcong proved, you don't have to be big to win a war these days, because the machinery does it for you. But you get used to one breed, so it's hard to get used to a new one. The Marines lined up on the dockside in Beirut were a motley crew: men with pot guts, short ones, tall ones, a lot with big thick glasses. Who knows, they probably all shot like Gary Cooper in *Sergeant York*; but the overwhelming impression was that the line-up was what you would get if you emptied any large office-block in midtown Manhattan and ordered all the men between nineteen and forty-five to put on fatigues, flak jackets and helmets. If I'd been my Palestinian friend on the way to Hodedia, I would have felt pretty safe when I saw the first Foreign Legionnaire come over the horizon. But with the Marines it was not so reassuring; the best thing about them was, as Americans they were probably safe because the Israelis surely wouldn't fire through their best ally to hit fighters. Well, they wouldn't, surely?

If the Israelis have ever managed to convince American administrations about anything, it is that anyone connected with the Palestinian Liberation Organization is certainly not human, is almost certainly a total psychopath and is also very likely to be so contaminated with communicable diseases that standing downwind from one of these monsters when he exhales is certain to lead to the clap, palsy and yaws. Begin was able to draw out his extermination campaign in west Beirut by insisting that Philip Habib should not be allowed to talk to the Palestinians; Phil talked to Saeb Salam, the grand old man of orthodox Lebanese Muslim politics . . . and Saeb, immunized by years of mixing with the terrorists, passed on Phil's thoughts to one of Arafat's men . . . who asked Arafat what he thought; then Arafat passed on the message to Saeb who – presumably after having his hands washed by a security man and a careful gargle to remove the contamination – talked to Phil, who passed on the thought to Begin's men. This system won whole days for the Israelis to knock off hundreds more civilians – far more than they could have blown away if Phil had simply called up Arafat and said, 'Yasser, this is what we've got for you today.' The belief that P.L.O. men carried communicable diseases and would also steal your wallet if they got close enough was drilled into every American Marine in the port area but as the hour approached for these creatures to descend on the port the Marines were guarding, their commanders were faced with the dreadful realization that they knew very little about how the evacuation was going to be carried out. Clearly, the crafty Palestinians, whose men were grouped outside the entrance to the port, would know when their men were likely to arrive and in how many trucks and by what route . . . but how was this information to be obtained? It would be undignified to ask reporters to go and ask the Palestine Liberation Army commanders, and downright degrading to have to pass messages through the Foreign Legion, but how else was it to be done? Was talking to a Palestinian the sort of initiative that could be taken on the ground by a regimental commander, or was this a question that had to be satellited back to Washington to wait for an answer from the State Department or the Joint Chiefs? Someone obviously bit on the bullet anyway, and, no doubt hoping that nobody would tell Menachem Begin, authorized the first contacts to be made between U.S. Marines and the Palestine Liberation Army. Like the first earthman alighting from his spaceship to meet the first Venusian, small trim Lt.-Col. Robert Johnson stepped over the line dividing his port area from the unknown world of west Beirut and cautiously shook hands with Lt.-Col. Salah abu Zarad, the area commander of the P.L.A. It was observed by reporters present at the scene that, after touching the Palestinian hand, Colonel Johnson did not turn green and fall writhing in agony to the ground; however, later inquiries determined that Colonel Johnson had in fact been born in Edinburgh, Scotland, and was therefore very probably immune to the sort of contamination Americans could expect when coming into contact with the P.L.O.

Lt.-Col. Salah turned out to be a man with a keen sense of public relations; soon after, he pulled the sort of stunt absolutely guaranteed to make Ariel Sharon grind his teeth down to the gums. When the great movement of Palestinians began, Salah suddenly materialized out of the crowd next to Johnson and produced a winsome six-year-old boy dressed in a miniature Fateh uniform, complete with cap and Fateh badges. He was a good-looking, smiling lad named Yasser, and Johnson, the old softy, knelt beside him to chuck him under the chin. But as the colonel knelt, one of Salah's men jammed an A.K.-47 into the kid's left hand, and at the same time the boy lifted his right to make a triumphant V-sign. It was a picture taken by various photographers on the scene, although the brilliant sun was right behind this touching tableau and none of the pictures was of high quality. They'll turn up in the archives at some point and, no doubt, provoke a biblical broadside from Begin about American collaborationists.

As the momentous meeting of Palestinian and American was taking place by the port, so the first Palestinians were gathering acrosss town to begin yet another great pull-out; among the older men, you could find veterans who remembered being driven out of Palestine by the Jews in 1948 and by the Jordanians out of Jordan in 1971. Those other two great movements had been desperate retreats, but this was a different sort of departure; this one was taking place by choice, with soldiers carrying their guns with them; but sadness and apprehension were heavy in the air because the men who were leaving knew they would not be coming back, while the families they were leaving behind were terrified by the thought that they would be going back to camps stripped of their defenders. The two groups, the fighters and those they were leaving behind, met together for the last time on the football field of the Arab University in the heart of Palestinian west Beirut in the Fakhani district that had taken the worst shelling and bombing in the war. On that dusty ground, heavy with the scent of eucalyptus trees on the boundary of the playing area, men, women and children made their last farewells.

If you were in the news business, it was a T.V. or still cameraman's event. People who know they might be seeing each other for the last time – and I haven't any doubt that some of the women and children reaching out to their men in the big, green, two-and-a-half-ton trucks ended up in those piles of corpses in Chatila and Sabra – don't hide their emotions, nor do they have time or need to talk to journalists. Incredible pictures: teenage kids loaded with heavy packs, carrying rifles, wearing t-shirts with Yasser Arafat's portrait on the chest hugging mothers and young brothers and sisters before climbing on the trucks; white-bearded veterans with the old wooden-stock A.K.-47s hugging younger sons carrying the new A.K. with the folding metal stock; girl soldiers with *khaffiyehs* wrapped round their head, pistol stuck in belt, clinging on to their boyfriends before the trucks started to move. Palestinians are the only Arabs I know who are truly comfortable with women, who can hold them and hug them in public, joke with them and – as many a guerrilla raid has shown – fight with them and serve under them. Even the Lebanese, the most sophisticated of people at that end of the Mediterranean, have problems with what to do with women in public – I remember vividly when at some break in the civil war, the first Middle East Airlines plane for about five months flew into Beirut Airport and a vast crowd surged forward on to the tarmac to greet the incoming passengers. What remains freshest in my memory of that meeting was all the men hugging and kissing the other men, then turning and shaking hands politely with the women. Someone, Bassam or Mahmoud Labady probably, once told me, 'If you're good enough to fight and die for the revolution, you're good enough to be treated as an equal,' or something like that; with the Palestinians, it works that way; in the martyrs' cemetery you will see the faces of teenage girls staring from the photographs on their tombstones intermingled with pictures of the young men who were good enough to die for the revolution. So when you're leaving your women behind – or, for that matter, when your women are leaving you, because there were women fighters in the trucks as well – you hug them and kiss them and your tears mix and streak the dust on your face. Reluctantly they climbed on to the trucks, some wrapping themselves in the green-white-red-and black flag of Palestine, others waving the banners of their organizations, many more carrying posters of their leaders – Arafat everywhere, George Habash, the men from Saiqa with pictures of Hafez al Assad. Even as the trucks started to move, kids and girls were clinging to fighters, hanging on to the rails, hugging, crying, kissing, wailing goodbye,

hanging on to a door with one hand, wiping away the tears with the other.

As the first trucks inched through the gates of the football ground, the guns began firing. This was a time when everyone in west Beirut from about the age of twelve upwards had an A.K. and it seemed everyone was going to fire a last salute to the departing warriors. As the trucks moved down Corniche Mazra'a, you were reminded of accounts of the great Arab crusades into Spain and western Europe in the fourteenth century. No horses and camels and warriors with swords this time, but the trucks and jeeps ablaze with colour, the multi-coloured Palestinian banners trailing in the breeze, green silk flags with Koranic verses on them, the scarlet banners of Marxist organizations like the Democratic Front, the men wrapped in checkered *khaffiyehs* brandishing their guns; around them, the mind-jarring chatter and boom of thousands of guns being fired into the air. The heavy rattle of the A.K.s, the lighter, quicker chatter of American M-16s, the jack-hammer thudding of heavy-calibre Dutchka anti-aircraft guns fired from the back of jeeps, even the pop of pistols as passers-by suddenly pulled ·38s and ·44s out of hip pockets and added their noise to the din. Hot spent cartridges rattled off my car as I drove through the throng, flinching every hundred yards or so as some kid who'd left his A.K. behind would suddenly fire an R.P.G. round, the rocket swooshing by the car, then exploding up in the air with a great crack and a puff of black smoke. Occasionally, through this cavalcade would flitter one of the little white Palestinian Red Crescent ambulances, sirens howling and white-coated nurses screaming through the windows, rushing people wounded by flying bullets to hospital. I remember approaching a bridge through this firestorm when a man ahead of me raised his A.K. aloft and fired a triumphant burst and, in a scene that was pure Laurel and Hardy, fell, half-stunned by lumps of concrete broken off by bullets smashing into the underside of the bridge ten feet above his head. I followed several of these processions but even on days when I was caught on the other side of town, I would know they were coming as the waves of sound grew louder and louder and the puffs of black smoke of exploding R.P.G. rounds got closer. And if every man along the street was firing some sort of gun into the air, so every second woman would be throwing flowers, or sprinkling the fighters with rose-water and grains of rice as they passed.

Colonel Johnson had told us that a lot of his young Marines were under twenty years old and had not seen action of any kind before. They were told that there would be some sort of celebration when the fighters left; but no briefing could have prepared them for what was now about to burst on them. The booming and banging was getting closer and all of us, soldiers and reporters and sightseers, all turned to watch that point on the road where the fighters' convoy would first come into view. This was at the top of a small hill, which had once been covered with the old Turkish-style buildings of the commercial centre, but which was now strewn with ruins left by the civil war. The ruins were of golden stone; lit by the morning light and seen against the brilliant blue sky, they looked as if they had been like that for a thousand years. As we watched, the firing died away as the approaching procession turned into a street hidden from us; the intervening buildings filtered out the sound and, for a minute or so, our little hollow became so quiet that a hawk suddenly dipped down and started to hover over the broken stones where the lizards were warming themselves in the early sun.

Then the great caravan burst upon us, announcing its arrival at the top of the rise with a barrage of rifle-fire, the heavy crack of the rocket-launchers and the dull boom of a group of artillery pieces on the seafront. The trucks, filled with fighters, were preceded by a flock of cars and jeeps loaded with teenage boys and girls firing A.K.s in the air and scattering hand-grenades out of the windows the way Johnny Appleseed once threw apple-pips. A wild-eyed kid in a Yasser Arafat t-shirt standing within fifteen yards of the Marines started firing bursts from the A.K. he held in one hand and punctuating them with shots from the ·38 he held in the other – a hair-raising exercise because there is enough recoil from an A.K. to make it swirl all over the place if it is held in only one hand. One of the leading jeeps had a loudspeaker, and some girl was screaming, '*Allahu Akbar*,' at full volume; this noise had to compete with a circle of middle-aged Palestinian women standing with the journalists who were all crying together, '*Thawra, thawra, hatta an nasr*,' which someone translated as 'Revolution, revolution until victory'. Then the first truck, with banners waving, finally appeared; the uproar increased by a factor of five as everyone but the Marines and the Foreign Legionnaires surged into the roadway, firing pistols and rifles, throwing grenades, loosing off rockets and howling war-chants and victory slogans. In the middle of this seething mass of people, the little Yasser suddenly reappeared, holding in front of him an enormous gold-plated ·45 automatic. He was yanking on the trigger of the thing and waving it around at crotch height – I can only assume that nobody got hit because the safety catch was on, or the kid didn't have the strength to pull the trigger.

That blustering bully Sharon was quoted on Israeli radio as saying that the departure of the Palestinians was 'one of the greatest achievements in Israel's history'. Well, bullshit to that, for starters. Even if his very reluctant army had managed to sort itself out to the point of actually getting into west Beirut and forcing the Palestinians out with their hands over their heads, they wouldn't have achieved much – after all, they out-numbered the Pals about five to one in men, and had infinitely superior weaponry at every level – so total victory was the very least they could honourably have achieved as a military force. As it was, they all went out with their guns in their hands and the cheers of the crowd ringing around them, past that final sign at the dockside that read 'Beirut will never forget'; and more than anything, they knew they were going, not because they had to, but because the leaders had decided that the time had come to move out and live to fight another day. Since then, I have had the usual arguments about who won what; so far, I have not found anyone who could satisfactorily answer this question: 'Tell me, do you think Menachem Begin got 500 of his guys killed and blackened Israel's name throughout the world and spent two billion dollars, just so that Yasser Arafat could take a luxury cruise to Greece?'

9
Weaving Nightmares

'I was one of the Christian gunmen on that Palestinian shoot down Sabra and Chatila way in September last year, and all I can say is, I cannot imagine what all the uproar is about. As these hunts go, it was nothing out of the ordinary at all, very much like the drive in Karantina in 1976 when we got a very good bag of Kurds. The camps were like Karantina because they were very much of a fun thing: a few days out in the open air and a good bag to show at the end of it. Nothing at all like Tal Zaatar, I can tell you, because Tal Zaatar took for ever, and it was bloody dangerous as well. If you like comparisons, Sabra and Chatila were like a pheasant shoot; Tal Zaatar was like a tiger hunt, much more exhausting and dangerous, but much more rewarding. Not that Sabra and Chatila didn't bring you out in a healthy sweat of course, because you have to run like hell to catch those bloody ten-year-olds – they move like rabbits when they see old grannie with her head half off. All in all, an entertaining few days after sitting around for two months doing nothing while the Israelis had all the fun; I'd forgotten how much enjoyment you can have, picking off a nippy teenager on the run. And easy for the Palestinians as well – I doubt if one in ten felt a thing.

'But the fuss, the uproar, the breast-beating! If we'd shot a load of human beings, it couldn't have been any worse. Television cameras all over the place, reporters saying it was the worst thing to happen in the Middle East since the fall of Byzantium, and those bloody Israelis leaping up and down in a frenzy, saying *they* had nothing to do with it, and it was all *so* unexpected, and deary me, how could people *do* such dreadful things to innocent civilians.

'Well, bugger me with the rough end of a pineapple, the Israelis of all people asking how we could do it! We do a little bit of tidying up at the end of their season, clean up the ground after they've had their fun on it . . . and they start doing their nuts. Can you imagine they could have the gall to ask how we could do what we did! They spend two months bombing and shelling those camps every day; they use cluster-bombs and incendiaries and phosphorus shells; they leave kids with their guts split open and their legs sliced off; they burn old men and women to death; they leave people in the ruins of their houses, watching the smoke rise from their chests as the phosphorus burns through to their lungs; they cut off their food and water supplies – then they say they can't understand why we wanted a share in the fun. That murderous oaf Sharon, up to his guts in blood, has the outstanding nerve to stand in front of his own commission of inquiry and say, perfectly straight-faced, "These atrocities stand in contradiction not only to the values towards which we were educated and which we teach . . . we were surprised, astounded and shocked by the massacre that took place in those neighbourhoods in Beirut." '

I wrote the last few lines in a fine rage, thinking that irony was the only way to try to express what I feel about what the Israelis did in Beirut in 1982. The fury was on me because the buggers are going to get away with what they did, and the reason they will is that the massacre at the finish completely wiped out the memories and indignation about what had gone on before the killings in the camps. If I'd been doing public relations for the Israeli army I couldn't have thought of a more brilliant scheme to get them off the hook than having those last few hundred people killed in the camps. As soon as the news leaked out, the whole of the world's attention was focused on Sabra and Chatila and away from the butchers of Beirut. Suddenly the villains were the Christian militiamen; and attention was distracted even more by the question whether it was Haddad's people or Gemayel's Phalangists. The Israelis got a little mud splashed on them through guilt by association, because whoever did the killings couldn't have done them without the Israelis opening the way. But compared with the real weight of condemnation they deserved for what they had done to Beirut, the confused and bewildered indignation over the camp killings was easy to deal with.

The fact is that the Israelis are as responsible for the deaths in the camps as they were for the deaths in the war, just as a Nazi commander would be judged guilty of mass murder, even if he had just stood by while his Ukrainian *Einsatzgruppe* slaughtered the Jewish peasants in the town his troops had first broken open. In the two months of the siege the Israelis established that everyone in west Beirut was a legitimate target; they hit every part of the city, using the vilest of modern weapons and showing absolutely no concern for the lives of civilians; more than anything, their obsessive shelling of camps like Sabra and Chatila showed they considered the people who lived in these areas had even less right to live than the other citizens of the city.

Whatever you might say of them, the Christian militiamen are not ignorant, unthinking peasants. They read the reports coming out of west Beirut every day, they heard the Palestinian and Muslim militiamen's radio broadcasts about what was happening in west Beirut. They knew it was open season on purely civilian areas; they knew the Israelis were deliberately terrorizing west Beirut. The Israelis were responsible for the climate of mindless violence and the downgrading of human life to less than nothing in west Beirut. Nothing the Christians did in the camps was in any way more reprehensible than what the Israeli armed forces had done for two months preceding the final massacres.

I find it much easier to understand what the Christians did in the camps than what the Israelis did to west Beirut. I was in Beirut during the civil war and although I was not in Damour, I know how Christian families were butchered there. Both sides committed atrocities, although, in terms of the mathematics of horror, the Christians have more to answer for: Karatina, Tal Zaatar, Jisr al Basha and now Sabra and Chatila, as against Damour and Jiyeh. I name these alone, because nobody has ever tallied the individual acts of brutality that left the eyeless corpses under the Fuad Chehab flyover, the burnt bodies on either side of the crossing-points between east and west. However, because of the civil war there is hardly a family on either side in Lebanon that does not remember the violent death of a relative or friend. The Christian gunman carefully lining up the six-year-old girl in his sights in Sabra may have remembered a tragedy of his own as he created another. I would feel much more comfortable with such a man – as I would with a Palestinian who throws a grenade into a school in a *kibbutz* – than I ever would with an Israeli bomber-pilot or commander of an artillery crew . . .

This is not to say that I support what any of them are doing; but the man who stares down the barrel or pulls the pin has to make the decision to kill someone, he must watch them die, he has to live with that vision for the rest of his life and almost invariably with the Palestinian, he knows he will soon die because of what he has done. The pilot or the soldier pulling the lanyard on a howitzer performs an action no more stressful than ringing a doorbell; if his co-ordinates are anywhere near right he does ten times the damage and causes fifty times the misery of any half-baked little 'terrorist', yet he never hears a scream or sees a tear or has to watch blood spurt. He will sleep peacefully every night of his life because there is no raw material for his conscience to weave into nightmares.

There is no national memorial to the victims of the civil war in Lebanon, no place where you can see the pictures, the documents and the artefacts to remind you of what man is capable of doing to his fellow men when the rule of law is suspended. There is in Jerusalem; it is called Yad Vashem, and it records what happened to the Jews of Europe in the Holocaust. I remember going there once, so long ago that very few memories remain, but those that do are very strong. The most haunting images from that place are the pictures of the children waiting to go to the camps. They stare at you from the photographs, those long-dead children, not so much terrified, because they didn't know what was going to happen to them, as apprehensive because they have sensed the mood of the adults around them, they have seen the faces of their parents and neighbours and of the German guards standing over them. You feel most moved by the plight of the children because of their utter helplessness. Your pity for the adults is tempered just that tiny fraction because maybe, just maybe, some of them might have escaped if they had reacted a little faster, left when they first watched the rise of the Nazis, got out rather than staying because they believed their Aryan friends would protect them. You cry for the children because they never even had a choice.

You walk through those dimly lit rooms in that long low building on the hillside in Jerusalem, wondering at how little there is to see: the few pairs of striped concentration-camp pyjamas, the handful of yellow stars, the yellowing pages of anti-semitic newspapers, a pathetic collection of identification documents with '*Jude*' stamped on them. You come out past the flickering flame in the room whose floor bears the names of the concentration camps, and you wonder that the destruction of six million people was so thorough that it left hardly more tangible reminders of their existence than a single middle-class family might accumulate in its lifetime.

One other memory of Yad Vashem remains with me, and that is how deserted it was. I had gone there on a weekday in miserable weather (it was, I think, January or February) and it was cold and the rain was slanting

Israel looks on

down, showering off the leaves of the trees lining the roadway up to the memorial. I'm not quite sure what I expected, but I thought somehow there would be school groups, perhaps students from religious schools, older local people and foreign tourists but the place was almost totally deserted, no groups of people at all, just a few couples, single wanderers like myself, occasionally knots of four or five American tourists and virtually no Israelis. It might simply have been one of those days when the weather was too bad for locals to come – after all, if you can visit a place any time, you don't make a journey through the rain to go there. But Yad Vashem was also a neglected place: the rooms echoed to the drip of rain-water falling through the cracked ceiling and into black plastic buckets scattered through the exhibition rooms. The large photographs were ragged and curling at the edges, the glass of the display cases was marked with fingerprints; at the exit, a man asked me to contribute to its upkeep. There was something in the feel of the place that I found when I visited the churches built by the British in India during the Raj: the regimental chapels in places like Lahore and Rawalpindi, with the brass plaques on the walls commemorating long-forgotten battles and equally forgotten soldiers. The places stand there, not so much abandoned as irrelevant.

I suppose it is simply too naïve to ask whether the Israeli cabinet ministers and generals who planned and put into operation the siege of Beirut are familiar with Yad Vashem and, if they are, whether it has left any memories. Have they ever looked at the commentaries beside those showcases that tell the history of the destruction of the Jews? First the violent press campaigns against them; then the administrative changes that removed the protection of the law; then the confiscation of property; and finally their physical destruction. I wonder if anyone drew any parallels between the Nazi cry that all Jews were usurers and bloodsuckers preying on the pure Aryans, and the obsessive use of the word 'terrorist' to describe Palestinians. I wonder if any of those leaders saw any parallels between the destruction of the Palestinian camps and attempts to terrify and starve the people trapped in west Beirut with the destruction of the ghettos in Eastern Europe. I wonder if anyone questioned whether there was much difference between using phosphorus shells against a hospital full of mentally retarded children and old people, and the murder of Europe's mentally ill. If it is morally unacceptable for a Stuka to dive-bomb the Warsaw ghetto, is it somehow defensible for an F-16 to bomb a purely Lebanese civilian district like Raouche? Was Yad Vashem built to remind the world of the evil man is capable of wreaking on his fellow men, or is it there to state that brute force can always snuff out a weaker people?

In the end, it comes down to the old question: who is the terrorist? If the Palestinian commando team that comes ashore from a rubber boat and blows up a bus and its passengers near Tel Aviv is a group of terrorists, what is the group of Israeli soldiers standing by their howitzer on the hills outside Beirut that carefully selects a phosphorus shell and incinerates a family in their apartment in Fakhani? The commando team that gets into a school in northern Israel and shoots children is a terrorist group . . . so what are the pilots of a squadron who watch their armourers carefully loading the long grey pods of the cluster-bombs that they will soon be dropping near the Acca Hospital where the Palestinian and Lebanese refugees must bring their wounded every day?

Towards the end of the siege, I remember going to watch the release of Aharon Ahiaz, the only Israeli pilot shot down in the war. He had piloted an American Skyhawk fighter-bomber that normally delivers a bomb-load of about four tons. I saw the results of strikes like that all over Beirut: I remember especially seeing one in a middle-class district in Raouche, where a building had collapsed on a family; and watching a dead thirteen-year-old girl being dug out of the wreckage. Her blood, soaked into the dust and earth, had dried and hardened so that when the body was finally lifted out of the earth, it looked like a piece of ancient treetrunk, until suddenly you saw one quite clean white hand at the end of what otherwise might have been a fractured branch. Just in case Mr Ahiaz should read this and think of sueing, let me say I do not know whether his plane was carrying any weapons at all when it was shot down; he may have been on a photo-reconnaissance trip or, for all I know, had a full load of chocolate candy to drop on the camps to cheer up the kids cowering below him. Far be it for me to accuse him of driving a fighter-bomber over Beirut with murder in mind . . . I'm sure it was not in his mind at all, it was all the other guys who did it.

Aharon Ahiaz was a blond curly-haired man of about thirty-five, wearing a dark blue patterned shirt straining over a marked paunch. He was laughing and joking with a Palestinian guard and he smiled at us pressmen as he waited until the car came to drive him away to freedom. He had been a prisoner for almost the length of the siege and the Palestinians had gone to enormous lengths to make sure he wasn't hurt in the bombing that devastated the area. As I watched him driving away, I had a sudden flashback to a T.V. news programme of three or four years earlier about a commando raid in Israel in which three or four Palestinians had taken over a school and (as I recall) had shot several of the pupils. They were holed up in the schoolhouse and in the end, the Israelis made one of their usual storming attacks on the building and shot the Palestinians. I remember watching as the guerrillas' bodies were dragged out into the schoolyard and the hysterical crowd started kicking and spitting on the corpses, screaming and rolling the bodies in the dust in rage and anguish.

I asked Bassam abu Sharif once whether he thought

acts of terrorism were morally justified. He had been named again and again by the Israelis as one of the masterminds of P.F.L.P. terrorist operations in the past and is high on their hit-list; sitting with him in the open is always a slightly spooky experience because they have tried more than once to get him – and he has the scars to prove it. He said that in the end, there could be no justification at all for straight-out terror attacks; but then he thought a little more and said, 'That is not to say we haven't carried out such operations, and I wouldn't try to justify them to you. All I would say is, if you are going to apportion blame, then the Israelis have committed a hundred times more atrocities than we have. Compared to them we are very little terrorists indeed.'

It is no coincidence that when the Israeli forces began to question just what they were doing in Lebanon, it was not the pilots and the sailors who began to protest, to join in the peace demonstrations, and finally to refuse to go on with the butchery. I haven't read all the reports out of Israel from that period, but I would be astonished to read that there were in the navy and air force men like Colonel Eli Geva, the army officer who led the attack on Sidon. He was one of the most brilliant commanders in the Israeli army and he resigned, saying, 'I don't have the courage to look bereaved parents in the face and tell them their son fell in an operation which in my opinion we could have done without.'

The soldiers on the ground wouldn't need to have been to Yad Vashem to know what unopposed military force can do to a practically defenceless people. It was the soldiers who resigned and protested, because they were the ones who had to march through the ruined towns and villages, who had to see the bodies of the women and children, who could hear the screaming and crying of the bereaved. What honour the Israelis did salvage from the war lay in the actions of the men who said 'No more', after they had seen what they had done, or what had been done in their name. For the pilots and the sailors of course, there was nothing to remind them how sordid wars can be: no cries, no stink of rotting corpses, no dust and flies and blood. Sit back in air-conditioned comfort at 20,000 feet, press the tit and feel the plane lift as the bombs fall away, and back home in time for dinner without even getting wet under the arm-pits. Or for that matter, sit out enjoying the sea breezes, focus on that smoking cityscape across the sun-flecked waters and let the computer digest the co-ordinates and do the firing. Marvellous way to get a suntan and a damn sight less dangerous than driving through the holiday traffic to get the same sort of tan in Eilat.

Just before he left to go to Syria, I asked Mustafa what he thought would happen to the P.L.O., whether it would keep up the search for the solution that Arafat wanted, a political negotiation to get a homeland. I said that it would probably be a long-drawn-out process but if the Palestinians turned back to guerrilla operations as

many of the fighters wanted, then they would alienate world opinion. I suspect that he wondered how I could ask a question like that after sitting through the previous six weeks because he asked me, 'When has pleasing world opinion brought us anything? World opinion means nothing, and you know it because the world has been protesting about this siege in Beirut for the past two months, and yet the world has done nothing to stop the fighting. If we have learnt anything from Israel since June, it is that world opinion is meaningless and that to achieve anything – whether it be your freedom or to have your land – you have to carry a gun. You know as well as I do that we would all be dead or in Israeli jails by now if we hadn't fought. Don't talk to me about world opinion.'

Leaving aside the seventy-five Israeli soldiers who died when their headquarters in Tyre blew up, more Israelis (ninety-eight soldiers, by the end of February 1983) have been killed by Palestinian guerrillas since the end of Operation Peace For Galilee than were killed in the five years before this great crusade against 'the organizations of terror of the P.L.O.' – the official Israeli figure is fifty-three civilians and forty-three soldiers. I dread it, but I know that one day quite soon I will turn on the television and see the film from some-where in Israel, and the announcer will be saying that a Palestinian suicide squad has just commandeered a bus, or taken over a school or an airport, and then there will be the final shoot-out. First, there will be the screaming and crying of the friends and relations as the Israeli dead are carried away and later the bodies of the commandos will be dragged out. And then one of the Palestinian organizations will claim responsibility and publish one of those pre-raid pictures that always seem to be taken. There will be the three or four kids, maybe waving their A.K.-47s in the air, maybe standing, smiling into the camera with arms over each other's shoulders. And I won't want to see that picture because I know too many of the fighters now, and one day I'm going to be looking at someone who cared for me in Beirut in the summer of 1982.

No Israeli civilian deserves to die a random death like that, just as no young Palestinian should be forced into the belief that only the gun will win him his rights. Yet as I finish writing this book at the end of February 1983, I can see no sign that Israelis and Palestinians are going to stop killing one another this year. The killing will go on because the Palestinians will not get a homeland this year; it will go on until they do get one, or until there are no Palestinians left alive.

I want that last paragraph to be the one that makes me a laughing-stock. I want any critic who might see this book to be able to write a few lines that will go something like this: 'As an observer of a scene, Mr Clifton has certain qualities, but his book was spoilt by a last chapter which made the ludicrous prediction that the Pales-tinians would not get a homeland in 1983. As we all know, 1983 was the year when Menachem Begin bowed to American pressure and gave up the West Bank to the Palestinian people' (or I would be just as happy with '1983 was the year when Menachem Begin confounded the world, and won his second Nobel Peace Prize, by returning the West Bank' . . . and so on). 'The peace between the two new neighbours is a fragile one, we know, but it does exist.'

How can I hope for that sort of humiliation when I read today's newspapers? The settlements on the West Bank are scrambling up the ancient hillsides and the Israelis are telling the Lebanese they want heavily armed and fully manned bases across southern Lebanon for an unlimited time in the future; their old paranoia is rising again, this time – for God's sake – they are accusing the American Marines of allowing the Palestinians to operate across American lines. The significance of their latest protests is not that they are accusing the Americans but that less than six months after 'one of the greatest achievements in Israel's military history' the fighters are back making a mockery of the very name of Operation Peace For Galilee. Add another character to the group in Baha's joke; make him follow Reagan and Brezhnev and Arafat, and make him either an Israeli or a Palestinian. Then have him say: 'When are Jews and Palestinians going to stop killing each other in the Holy Land?' And use the same punchline.